THE MORAL OF THE STORY

A Storyteller's Guide to Helping Brands Build Relationships with People

Let your moral guide you.

Jeff Freedman

ISBN: 197753001X

ISBN 13: 9781977530011
Library of Congress Control Number: 2017915558
CreateSpace Independent Publishing Platform
North Charleston, South Carolina

In this book, I have tried to recreate events, locales, experiences, and conversations to the best of my memory. In some instances, I have changed or removed the names of individuals in order to protect their anonymity.

In memory of my friend and business partner,
Michael Connell.
Thank you for your everlasting inspiration and guidance.

PREFACE

Why do people fall in love with certain brands? Most often it is not because these brands have superior products or services, or because they provide the best value. In fact, these brands often demand premium prices for slightly above-average products. Yet audiences flock to these brands, speak positively about them, and repeatedly purchase from them—even after they make mistakes.

This book is intended to help you build those types of relationships.

Brands are as strong as the relationships they build. I witnessed this firsthand when my business partner, Mike, was battling cancer, and we were struggling to keep our advertising agency alive. Ultimately, it was our relationships that enabled us to not only survive but thrive during a very challenging time. But unfortunately, Mike did not.

After Mike passed, I started a nonprofit organization and cancer fund-raiser, and in doing so, I discovered that traditional marketing approaches are not designed to build relationships with people, especially in today's fully connected social media world. I, along with my colleagues, studied the world's most beloved brands to identify how they behave and why people so adored them. We found that they all shared one unique quality—a core belief that guided everything they did and was embedded in virtually every aspect of their business. We called it the moral of the story.

Since that time, I have been working with brands across all industries to identify the morals of their stories and use them to build strong relationships with people.

In this book, I share my personal soul-searching experience in which I discovered the true power of relationships and how great brands build them. Based on my experience of working with brands across all industries, I demonstrate how to discover the moral of your brand story. Then I share methods for sharing the moral with your audience to become a brand people love.

Enjoy.

ACKNOWLEDGEMENTS AND CREDITS

Special thanks to my wife, Jane, and children, Julia and Josh, for their unconditional love and support. To the entire team at Small Army for helping to bring the moral of the story to life for Small Army, Be Bold, Be Bald!, and all our clients. To all our amazing clients, many of whom are included here, for their ongoing trust and confidence. And to all my family members, friends, and colleagues who are a part of my story. Thank you.

Cover Illustration & Design:	Brandon Brown
Editing:	Francesca Grossman
Author photograph:	Keirnan Klosek, KCK Photography

TABLE OF CONTENTS

SECTION ONE

Soul-Searching

CHAPTER 1
PERSPECTIVE

It was the day after Christmas 2005. I was with my wife and two-year-old daughter at our cabin in the backwoods of Maine. The office was closed for the holiday week, and I was trying to decompress after completing the third year of our advertising agency, Small Army.

It had been quite a ride. After working together for many years at another agency in Boston, my friend Mike and I had decided to venture out on our own. Seeing that the tech bubble had just burst and ad agencies were dropping like flies, it seemed a bit crazy. But despite what our wives suggested, we thought it was a good idea. We knew we'd make a great team and dreamed of building an agency that could endure anything, so we marched forward.

Three years later, we were being recognized as one of the top twenty agencies in Boston, doing work with some of the most respectable brands in the region, and attracting amazing talent to work for us. And we had just moved into new space on Newbury Street, right across the street from The Ritz-Carlton and next to the Public Garden, preparing for continued growth and success.

As I sank into the worn blue couch in the family room and stared out the window onto the snow-covered lake, I could sense my mind clearing and my entire body relaxing. I was enjoying my sanctuary. Then the phone rang. If not for the caller ID reading "Michael Connell," I would have just let it go. But I never let an opportunity to speak with Mike pass me by.

I hit the answer button, put the phone to my head, and merrily greeted my friend, "Hey, Mike. Merry Christmas!"

"Hey, buddy." I loved when Mike called me that. If you knew Mike, you'd know how cool it was to be his buddy.

Immediately, I could sense something was wrong. We knew each other incredibly well. When you start a business with someone, you spend a lot of time together—often more time than you spend with your wife and kids. Almost every waking moment, we were side by side—planning, debating, collaborating, and building together, so just the slightest shift in the tone of his voice told me something wasn't right.

"What's wrong?" I asked him.

"Well, probably not a big deal or anything," he said with his usual confidence that anyone else would have taken as real. "You know that lump in my throat that they were supposed to remove last week? Well, they didn't remove it. They did some tests and found that I have cancer again."

"What?" I get emotional fairly quickly, and that was about all I could get out of my mouth. Mike had had cancer twice before—Hodgkin's—but he had beat it and had now been cancer free for more than fifteen years. I didn't know him back then, and never really knew anyone who had battled cancer before, so this was all new territory for me. And from all I knew or heard about it, I could only imagine the worst.

He continued. "They need to start treating it right away. Right after the baby is born, I'll need to start chemo."

Mike had two young kids—a boy and a girl. His daughter and mine were the same age. I remember when Mike pulled me into our conference room on South Street in Boston, after we'd been in business for less than one year. With a big smile, he sat down on a chair in our makeshift meeting room and pointed at the other chair for me to do the same.

"I have some news to share with you. We're having another baby," he said.

I gave him a huge hug and then replied, "Congratulations! We're having a baby too." Seems like we really did do everything together.

Now, Mike and his wife were expecting the arrival of their third child—another little boy—later that week.

"That soon?" I asked, beginning to understand the severity of the situation.

"Yeah. It's stage four, so they need to move quickly. I'll be fine. I've been through this before. Don't worry, buddy. Everything will be OK."

"OK. I'll talk with you soon."

I hung up the phone and immediately burst into tears. I knew there was still a lot we needed to talk about, but I couldn't talk. I didn't know what to do.

I don't quite know what emotions ran through me. Of course I was sad, but mostly I think I was scared. Scared for Mike. Scared for his family. And scared for the business.

Mike was more than just my business partner. He was my friend, cheerleader, mentor, inspiration, and greatest source of confidence. To this day, hanging on the wall of my office is a note from Mike on our original Small Army letterhead, dated November 8, 2002. It reads:

Jeff,
I think it's only fitting that my first official correspondence on the thrilling new Small Army stationery be a note to tell you how glad I am that we're doing this and what a pleasure it is working

with you. These past few months have been a blast, and I know that we're onto something big here.

To the (lucrative) future of Small Army!

Mike

He just had a way of making me feel great about myself and the work we were doing together. About two years after starting the agency, we moved offices to Boylston Street in Boston—right at the finish line of the Boston Marathon. Mike and I both drove into town each day and parked our cars in the Copley Mall garage. We would often bump into each other in the morning and almost always walked back to our cars together at the end of the day. One morning, while walking together, I was telling Mike about a meeting I had the previous day in which the client was very excited about the work I presented. I remember saying, "Mike, we're like a real company." He quickly corrected me, "Jeff, we *are* a real company." It was always difficult for me to see that, but Mike always made sure I did.

He was also the creative leader of the business. The lead storyteller. The star of the show. In meetings, as I would present research findings and strategic insights, clients would anxiously tap their fingers on the table as though their movements would take them to the creative part of the presentation more quickly. Rather than looking at the charts and graphs I painstakingly put together, they stared at the pile of storyboards sitting facedown in front of Mike, wondering with anticipation what lay beneath. They wanted to see how we were going to tell their story—and Mike always showed them that with incredible grace. Everyone in the room would be mesmerized as, one by one, he picked up the boards, handling each as though it were a Monet or Rembrandt. As he shared the insight behind what was about to be revealed, you could practically see the drool coming out of people's mouths in anticipation. It was not only a presentation, it was a performance. And Mike was a master.

On the morning we returned from holiday break, we gathered everyone around the table in the small conference room overlooking Newbury Street. Mike gave everyone big hugs as they walked into the room—not in preparation for the news, but simply because he hadn't seen them in more than a week. That was just what he did. He truly loved and cared for these people and acted accordingly. Under usual circumstances, I would have done the same, but I knew that a hug would squeeze my emotions right out of me, and I'd become a crying wreck. I stayed seated and tried not to make too much eye contact with anyone. There was lots of small talk about what people had done over the holidays as we waited for the last few people to arrive. But people were only half listening to one another, as they could sense something was going on and were trying to discern any hints of the news about to be shared.

As soon as everyone arrived, Mike began to speak. I knew that if I even tried to talk, I would break into tears, so as usual, Mike took the helm and shared the news. As he told the team the details of his situation and the plans for his treatment, tears streamed down everyone's faces.

Somehow, regardless of how many people were in a room, Mike was able to make everyone feel he was speaking directly to him or her. As he looked into each of our eyes, he assured us with complete conviction, "Don't worry, guys. It's gonna be fine. I've been through this before. It'll just be a few months or so, and then I'll be back. And when I'm getting treatment, I'll still be available. I'll be right downtown, and I'll come here afterward whenever I can."

I still cannot understand how he was able to maintain such composure and confidence in that situation. He was the one about to fight cancer, yet he was consoling us.

As I looked around the room, I worried about how long each team member would stick around. I knew their tears were for

Mike, but I knew they were also thinking about what this meant for their own futures. They knew, as I did, that Mike was the star of the agency and worried about how his absence could impact us. I feared this was just the beginning of the end.

After the all-agency meeting, we began telling friends and clients—and it didn't take long before word of Mike's illness spread throughout the community. I feared how others would react. Our clients would surely begin looking elsewhere, and other agencies, sensing our upcoming demise, would surely begin reaching out to our employees and clients to "save" them. This is how this business works—people and clients move around from agency to agency, and this would seem like the perfect time to move on.

But a strange thing happened.

Within days, I was inundated with calls and e-mails from people in the industry—many of whom I only knew through Mike—offering to come in and help out. With each offer came a story about Mike. How he had impacted their lives. How he had helped them in a difficult time. How he had made them laugh. How he had helped them in their career. Or just how he was always a true friend.

One friend in particular, Paul Norwood, offered to serve as our interim creative director while Mike went through his treatment. He had been with Mike through his cancer treatment years earlier and was prepared to help him through it again.

Paul was a founding partner at Cohn Godley Norwood (CGN), where Mike and I first met. Mike served as co-creative director with Paul, and I was the head of media and interactive services. But Paul's relationship with Mike went back much further than that. Earlier in their careers, they were creative partners at Cabot Advertising, a large ad firm based in Boston. Mike was a copywriter, and Paul was an art director—and together they were a creative force to be reckoned with. Their partnership resulted not only in countless awards, but also a deep personal friendship.

When Paul moved to California, the dynamic duo was temporarily broken up. But eventually Paul came back to Boston to launch CGN with a childhood friend, Ben Godley, and Rick Cohn—and it wasn't long before Paul brought Mike in to serve as his co-creative director.

With the Paul-and-Mike team back in place, CGN's success skyrocketed. In only five years, the agency grew from four to sixty people and was eventually sold in 1998 to a large direct-marketing company. Shortly after the sale, Paul left the advertising business and focused on his art, selling his work in galleries around the country. So when he offered to jump back in to help out, I was truly taken aback. Not only was he willing to help, he refused to take any salary for doing so. "I'm not doing this for a paycheck," Paul told me. "I'm doing this for you and Mike. This is what friends do for one another." Paul immediately gave me a sense of hope that we could possibly get through this.

We originally planned for Paul's tenure to be a few days each week over the next four to six months, when he would fill in while Mike was out getting treatment or resting. But he ultimately took on the role of interim creative director for almost two years (and I did eventually convince him to take some salary—albeit small).

Next was dealing with clients. With each client call, I was prepared to be given notice. If they let rationality lead their decisions, they should have left us. The one person they depended upon most to craft their story was about to be unavailable. There were plenty of other agencies they could have gone to—a few of which I had learned were actively calling them. But our clients ignored the pitches and stayed with us. All of them. They trusted us. They realized there might be some bumps in the road as we navigated the months ahead, but they were prepared for that.

"Jeff, we know this is a difficult time for you. But we know you and trust that you will figure it out," all the clients would tell me in their own words. "We're with you in this."

They were driven to help us as opposed to leave us. They not only stayed with us, but they gave us even more business and referred other clients our way. And when we messed up (which we often did), they forgave us.

With Paul at the creative helm, our team put in the extra effort. It was our responsibility to keep the agency—our dream—alive. It often meant long nights and weekends, but we did whatever it took to make sure we delivered.

The battle went on for two long years, with many ups and downs. The agency survived. But sadly, Mike didn't. On November 21, 2007, Mike lost his battle to cancer.

I often think back to that phone call in Maine as the moment my entire perspective on life and business shifted. My priorities changed. My view of advertising changed. And I began to respect and understand things in a way I had not quite done before.

I had always appreciated Mike's creative talent, but I often grew frustrated with the amount of time he would spend on seemingly nonproductive activities. Day after day, I would hear Mike laughing in his office. Employees would constantly be going in and out, spending hours on end listening to him spin long yarns and sharing more stories with him to add to his arsenal.

Client phone calls that should have lasted thirty minutes would end up lasting hours as he spent countless minutes sharing weekend adventures, kids' accomplishments, and other nonwork-related stories.

And the amount of *pro bono* work we did for charities he was involved with often made me cringe. How were we going to survive if we did work for clients who didn't pay?

Mike found it important to share his life with everyone, to know more about others' lives, and to offer help to anyone who needed it. This philosophy extended beyond clients, employees, and friends. Mike was often late to the office because he would stop to chat with the attendant in the parking garage or the security guard at the front desk of our building. I didn't even know their names, yet Mike knew where they lived, their kids' names, where they went to school, their life goals, and, probably, what they had for dinner the night before. At the holidays, he would bring them gifts, and he regularly gave them advice and guidance in life.

While part of me appreciated this kindness, another part grew more and more frustrated with the seemingly unfair fifty-fifty partnership. As I spent my twelve-hour days head down in spreadsheets and PowerPoint presentations, Mike was out yukking it up with everyone.

"I don't know if this is going to work," I'd often tell my wife after a long day at the office. "I love Mike, but it just seems so unfair."

But for the two years that followed that dreaded phone call, I realized our survival was not due to my complex spreadsheets and beautiful PowerPoint presentations. When I took an honest look back, I realized that the real reason for our survival—and our growth—was because of relationships. Relationships that Mike, more than anyone, took the time to build. Paul coming on to help us. Clients hanging in there with us. And employees not only staying with us, but also putting in the extra time and effort to fill the gaps. Every day, Mike built and nurtured these relationships with his seemingly endless stories, free work, big hugs, personal notes, and pure devotion to helping those around him.

In the top drawer of his desk, Mike kept a large box of personalized Crane stationary, which he regularly used to craft handwritten notes to people. Whether it was for a job well done, an important milestone, or a thank you, Mike always took the time to write a note to personally acknowledge people. Just like the handmade cards I get from my kids on my birthday or Father's Day, these notes were much more meaningful than any expensive gift. Now, in the top drawer of my desk, I have my stack of notes from Mike that I will forever cherish.

I used to believe that with talent and hard work, success would follow. That is why I thought Mike and I would create such a great agency. But I now realize that those two criteria are just the table stakes. Without them, you have little chance to succeed, but even when you have them, it is often not enough.

When you have strong relationships with people, they trust you. They listen to you. They forgive you for your faults. They introduce you to their friends. And they are there for you when you need them.

This is true for people, but it is also true for brands. When you have a relationship with a brand, you open their e-mails. You take their calls. When they make mistakes, you forgive them. You try their products and services when they come out—sometimes even waiting in lines overnight to buy them. And you often even pay more for their products—not because they are better, but because you find value in being associated with them. Why else would you pay so much for a coffee at Starbucks when you can get one for half the price anywhere else—or brew one at home for pennies?

As consumers, we are inundated with messages from thousands of brands every day. In fact, research studies consistently report that the average consumer is exposed to more than five thousand brands daily. Over 350 of those exposures are from ads—yet only about a dozen of those ads actually make an impression.

There are so many brands vying for our attention and our wallets, yet with each of them trying to scream over the other, all we tend to hear is the noise. It's not unlike being at a party with a few hundred people, all of them chatting. You may hear many of the voices, but together they become just a buzz in the background. The only meaningful words you hear are those of the people you take the time to be with: your friends, their friends, and perhaps a few other people who seem interesting enough to meet.

Mike didn't force people to listen to him or scream louder than everyone else to be heard—and people wanted to have a relationship with him. While his stories were always interesting, there was something much more profound that drew people to him. His soul shined through in everything he did. His contagious laugh. His big hugs. His personal notes and acts of generosity. His incredible strength and optimism in life. He did more than share stories with us, he shared his soul with us. That's also what great brands do.

CHAPTER 2
STORY

On November 14, 2007, my son, Josh, was born. As I sat on the bed in my wife's hospital room, my daughter on my knees, my son in my arms, and my wife's hand in mine, I couldn't have been happier. It was one of the happiest days of my life, but I was also filled with great sadness. At that exact moment, Mike was lying in a hospice bed, surrounded by his wife, children, family, and friends, waiting to take his final breath. I was torn. I knew I should be with my family during this time, but I also needed to be with Mike. I needed to be certain he knew how much I loved him and appreciated his friendship and partnership. I needed one more moment with him. I needed to say good-bye.

The day after sitting with my wife on her hospital bed, I was sitting next to Mike in his bed at the hospice. Unlike recent visits to his home or the hospital, there were no IV drips or other life-saving devices hooked up to his body. They were of no more use at this point—just painkillers to keep him comfortable and a monitor to know when he was gone. He calmly looked up at me, smiled, held out his hand, and asked to see a picture of Josh. I handed him my iPhone with photos of Josh at the ready, and, as he slowly mustered up enough energy to scroll through and examine each photo, he looked up at me and whispered, "He's beautiful." As he returned my phone, I took his hand in mine, looked into his eyes, and somehow got out the words "I love you." Mike, completely calm and, somehow, accepting of his fate, patted my hand softly and in his soft voice whispered, "Jeff, I know. It's OK."

As I left hospice, they told me they expected Mike to go at any moment. For days, I waited for the call. Fortunately, my house was chaotic, and I had lots to keep me occupied. My wife and Josh had just arrived home from the hospital. My in-laws were staying with us—in part to help out, but also for the upcoming celebrations. We were not only hosting Thanksgiving dinner at our house, but also preparing for Josh's bris on the day before Thanksgiving. According to Jewish law and tradition, on the eighth day after the birth of a boy, he is to be circumcised and blessed to officially become a Jewish boy. The one thought that kept going through my mind was what I would do if Mike's funeral and Josh's bris were on the same day. How could I possibly be absent at either one?

On November 21, 2007, with a small drop of wine in his mouth to calm the nerves and a slight twist of a knife, I witnessed my son begin his life as a Jewish boy. A few hours after the ceremony, I received the call telling me that Mike was no longer with us. Just as my son's life story began, Mike's came to an end.

At the funeral a few days later, I looked around at the hundreds of people sitting in the church pews. I couldn't help but think of Mike's life story. Amid all the sadness, it brought me some comfort.

Friends from his youth sparked visions of him cheering excitedly at NASCAR races and amateur wrestling matches. I thought back to the time Mike talked me into joining him and his buddies at a wrestling night at the Tsongas Arena in the old mill town of Lowell, Massachusetts, about thirty miles north of Boston. Mike and his friends had been going to matches together since they were kids growing up in small neighboring town of Westford, and they continued the tradition into adulthood. I was honored to be invited, taken under their wings as a student of the sport, and, most of all, welcomed into Mike's circle of longtime friends.

Looking out toward his creative colleagues, my thoughts shifted to scenes of Mike tossing ideas around conference rooms, shooting television commercials on beautiful ocean shores, and going on insight-finding expeditions to spark new ideas. I thought of Mike sharing his story of visiting Ground Round locations with Paul while they were working on the business at Cabot. They needed to learn more about the restaurant chain and its customers in order to come up with great creative ideas. I remember him telling me how at each stop, they would have something to eat and share a few drinks with the patrons at the bar. On one particular late-night stop at a location in the middle of nowhere, the patrons were intrigued by the "ad guys from Boston," and over the course of the evening, the entire crowd at the bar had gathered around to listen to their stories. After a few drinks too many, they decided to purchase some lottery tickets from the bar and jokingly told everyone that if they won, all the drinks would be on them. They won five hundred dollars and closed down the bar with their new friends.

Looking toward the young advertising professionals, I was reminded of the amazing mentor that Mike had been and how many people he had inspired and developed during his advertising career. I thought of all the times I sat with Mike during award shows, where he would whisper stories in my ear about each person he knew as he or she was called to the stage to be recognized. "I love that kid," he would often say with great pride, just as a teacher might say about a star student. I knew his creative talent would live on through all of them.

My colleagues at Small Army caused me, in part, to think about his struggle over the last two years—but also about his strength and perseverance during it all. The late nights and weekends ordering in food and working together to get things done. The hugs and tears we shared with one another. And the big wins that we achieved despite everything, including picking up the Bugaboo Creek Steak House account after a very challenging agency review. It may not have been the size of Ground Round, but it still made Mike proud.

Then I turned to his family, whom he loved and devoted himself to more than anyone else in the world. I couldn't imagine the pain his parents felt as they said good-bye to their son. That is not the order that is meant to happen. I looked at his oldest son, dressed like a young man in a jacket and tie. At only seven years old, he was about to become the man of the house. Mike's other two children sat in the pew with little understanding of what this truly meant for them. At only four and two years old, they would have few real memories of their father but would surely hear endless stories about him that would make them proud and help guide them into adulthood. And I looked at his wife, who had not only endured the pain over the last two years but was about to embark on a journey as a widow and single mom at such a young age.

Mike's life was a story, and each and every person in the church was one of the many characters in it. Some had major roles and some lesser ones. Some had been part of the story since the beginning, while others came into it much later. But everyone was part of it. Now, with streams of colored light shining through the stained-glass windows above, everyone gathered in this one great room for their final curtain call. Mike's story was over, but everyone involved will continue to share it forever.

Each of our lives is a story with a beginning and end, yet we almost never know when the ending will come or what may transpire along the way. Every decision we make can change the direction of our story. Every experience we have can change our perspective. Every person we encounter can make the story that much richer— and vice versa. I was a character in Mike's story—and he in mine— for less than ten years. And because of that, both our stories are richer.

Similarly, every brand has a story consisting of an endless string of characters and plot twists. Characters come and go with every change in leadership, employee promotion, staff layoff, customer win, merger, acquisition, and partnership. Every day brings new drama and plot twists. Lead characters such as CEOs and other executives make critical decisions that change the entire direction of the story—for better or worse. Evil villains such as competitors or hackers attack the brand with price reductions, sales promotions, employee poaching, and damaging viruses. Natural disasters come out of nowhere. Economic conditions change. Heroes come in and save the day with financing, turnaround strategies, and new business. And sometimes those same heroes are "killed off" by the board of directors, acquisitions, or in the case of Small Army, cancer.

You can't control everything that may happen in your life. But you can control how you respond to it. Every action Mike took, every response he made, every tale he told, and every relationship he built contributed to his story, and with each move it became even more interesting and compelling. People were attracted to it and excited to be a part of it. They stayed with it right until the end, and they will continue to share it forever.

Mike was an amazing storyteller, but he didn't tell his own story. He lived it. This is one of the many nuances that made Mike so special—and highlights one of the distinctions between brands you use and brands you love. The brands you love don't tell you how great they are. They show you how great they are. They live their story.

As a consumer, you are inundated with pitches from brands every day. But you tune them out. You pretend to be in a meeting or on another call when the sales representative calls on the phone. You delete dozens if not hundreds of e-mails every day from brands and individuals trying to get you to buy their products—often before you even open them. You barely notice the ads surrounding the content on the web page or mobile app you're engaging with—or you simply pay to block them out with ad blockers and premium apps so they won't annoy you. You don't answer the phone when the call comes in from the unknown number. You quickly scan past the ads in the magazine or newspaper and barely ever read the detailed copy the brand worked so hard to perfect. Unless it is the Super Bowl, you go to the bathroom, get a snack from the kitchen, or check your social-media feeds during the television commercials. And unless the solicitation is coming from a brand with whom you feel like you have a connection, you ignore it.

However, in moments of weakness, the print ad catches your attention. The radio spot draws you in. You take the phone call. Or you click on the ad. It happens. And more often than not, you regret your mistake. You're forced to listen to the long-winded sales pitch as to why you should give money to the charity, vote for the politician, purchase the book, make an appointment, download the thirty-day trial product, or visit the restaurant. And you believe none of it.

Research studies consistently show that consumers trust brands less than virtually any other source of information. You don't trust what brands tell you because you know they are just trying to sell you something. Instead, you trust word of mouth—especially from trusted sources. Years ago, before the Internet, Google, and social media, brands had an advantage. Word of mouth was not as accessible, so you were often dependent on brands for this information. You depended on them to tell you all about themselves, because it was difficult to get information elsewhere. But today, you can get it with a touch of a screen or click of a button. Do a Google search to find actual reviews and opinions from unbiased sources. Post a question about a brand or product category to your social network and have dozens of responses within moments.

Brand-marketing professionals often spend infinite amounts of time and resources crafting the story they want the audience to hear. They wrestle with the differentiators, unique selling points, and key messages that separate them from the competition. They spend weeks, and often months or years, working to perfectly craft a positioning statement and elevator pitch so everyone in their organization can clearly articulate who they are. Every word is thoughtfully considered to make sure it accurately represents the brand and appeals to anyone who might have a need for it.

I've seen companies literally spend hundreds of thousands of dollars to develop and communicate these statements. In fact, for many years, including some of the early years at Small Army, I confidently led many of these projects. We would hold long, intense sessions with brand executives, product managers, sales professionals, marketing execs, and others to listen to what made their products and services unique. They would debate their strengths and weaknesses and what their customers truly cared about. Each person would offer a different perspective based on the audiences they serve, the product or service they represent, or, more often than not, their most recent customer interaction. We would conduct surveys and speak with customers to learn what features, functions, and attributes they liked most about the brand and its products and how they were different from the competitors. We would also would carefully study the products and services of competitors—with detailed spreadsheets of attributes to identify and compare their strengths and weaknesses. After gathering all this valuable information, detailing what the brand does, who they do it for, how they do it, and what benefit it brings to the audience, we would carefully craft the perfect combination of words that would read something like this:

Brand X is a [type of company/category] that provides [benefit/reason to buy] to [target audience] who needs [what they need]. Unlike [alternatives/competition], Brand X [unique differentiator].

We were then prepared to share this perfect combination of words (and buzzwords) with each and every employee so they all had the ultimate elevator pitch for that moment when they were asked, "What is Brand X?" We created posters to hang in break rooms and conference rooms. We created tabletop pieces to put in company cafeterias. We drafted all-employee e-mails. We even updated employee IDs so the back of everyone's badge had the statement clearly written out. Company meetings and road shows were set up to announce the statement to everyone at the company. From that point forward, the positioning statement became the boilerplate on the end of all press releases, the opening to sales presentations, and the platform on which marketing communications were to be based.

However, even with all the marketing and promotion, few people ever follow the script. The statement may be written almost everywhere, but the actual words rarely come out of anyone's mouth. It sounds great in the boardroom, but outside of there, no matter how much you share it, no one ever remembers it. And on the rare occasion when employees do pull out the card to say it, they can feel their skin crawl with awkwardness as they recite it out loud.

People do not talk that way. And as you look the other person in the face, you realize the statement means little to him or her. In an attempt to create a statement that means something to everyone, you end up with one that means nothing to anyone.

This is not to say that a positioning statement is not valuable. The pieces of information within a positioning statement are important to know and communicate.

1. Who is our target customer?
2. How do we define our space/category?
3. What is the benefit we provide to our audience?
4. Who do we compete with?
5. How do we do things differently?

Each of these items is an important part of the story, but they are not the story itself—either individually or collectively. And whether you like it or not, they are all subject to change. Your brand story is a living, breathing thing that is constantly evolving over time. It changes every day—and often, it is out of your control. Existing competitors will one-up you with new products and services. New competitors will enter the market with completely new (and perhaps better) approaches to the customer need. The audience needs will evolve, and your products will do the same. Leadership will change. And this is just the tip of the iceberg.

Your brand story must be fluid, and those who are a part of the story must know more than how to tell it—they must know how to live it. Otherwise, the story will quickly get old and tired and, ultimately, will end.

Your brand story doesn't need a script. It needs a soul.

CHAPTER 3
SOUL

When the package from a local cancer center first landed on my desk in the winter of 2007, I assumed it had something to do with Mike. Since he had started his fight about fourteen months earlier, I received regular solicitations from cancer organizations asking for money or volunteer support. However, as I read through the contents of this package, I learned they were looking for something else: an agency to help create and manage a fundraiser for them.

Typically, for an RFP (request for proposal) like this, we would respond with our general capabilities, approach, and estimated fees. Unless the RFP was for a long-term relationship, we would not present creative ideas at this early stage—that would be like painting a family's house in order for them to hire you to paint their house.

However, with the potential to help an organization raise money to fight cancer, we decided to come up with a few different ideas to share with them in hopes of winning the business and having the opportunity to help.

As we would with any such assignment, we began learning about the cancer center, its audience, and the competition. We immediately recognized how many cancer fundraisers and relat-ed organizations are out there. Clearly we weren't alone in Mike's fight. However, as we looked more closely, we recognized that most of the fundraisers were similar—participants were sponsored to walk, run, or bike a set distance or route in honor of those who fight cancer. These events admirably attracted thousands of people and raised millions of dollars, but we struggled to see the meaning behind these events. We wanted to come up with an idea that not only could raise a lot of money but also had some sort of meaning and connection with the disease.

We knew the people most likely to participate in a fundraiser for a cancer-treatment organization were people just like us. They or someone they love had to battle cancer, and they want to do everything they could to honor them and strengthen their fight. So we asked ourselves, "What could we do to honor Mike and show him our support?"

We kept coming back to the same insight. When we spoke about Mike, we often spoke of his positive attitude and strength. Between doctor's appointments and treatments, he was rarely able to work. However, he was anxious to be involved and contribute. We laughed about Mike coming into the office after a treatment, excited to see everyone and help out, only to find him asleep in his office an hour later. Paul kept a stash of avocados in the refrigera-tor and would force Mike to eat them when he came in. "It's good fat," he would tell Mike, "and will give you energy." But Mike rarely had the appetite for them. On days Mike was feeling good, he'd call into the office and ask people to send him assignments or share work so he could review it and provide feedback. However, the good days were often followed by not-so-good days, so we'd of-ten have to present work to clients before Mike ever got back to us. But he tried so hard. And as often as he could, he would call me to check in. He'd ask about projects, clients, and of course, the team.

He'd coach me on how to handle different situations, remind me to acknowledge people for a job well done, and, without me even noticing, give me a pep talk to keep morale up and the ship moving forward. If you looked at his skinny body and bald head, you'd think he was weak, but he was stronger than any of us.

"How do we create something that honors this strength?" we asked one another. We found a few fundraisers where people raised money by shaving their heads, but we knew Mike would not want anyone to shave their head on his behalf. He never wanted people to feel bad for him—and definitely would not want people to shave their heads because of his hair loss. And how many people would really shave their head? we thought. Maybe some men would do it, but we would likely never get a critical mass of women to shave their heads.

"Why do we need people to shave their heads?" I challenged the team. "What if they just went bald for one day by wearing a bald cap?"

At first it seemed a bit crazy. But as we knew in the advertising business, great ideas are a bit crazy. We didn't need people to shave their heads. Instead, they could just wear a bald cap from the moment they woke up until the moment they went to sleep—and get people to sponsor them for doing so. Anyone could do it—male, female, child, adult, black, brown, or white. You didn't have to do any training, and you didn't have to travel anywhere to participate. Just put on the cap and go about your day as usual.

"I love it!" Mike responded when we shared the idea with him.

He also confirmed our thoughts about a head-shaving event, saying he would definitely not want people to shave their heads for him. But he found the bald-cap idea to be relevant and, at the same time, fun.

We wrote up the idea, sent it in with the RFP, and were sure we would get the business.

About one week later, we heard back from the organization. They hated the idea. They said there was no way they would ever do an event like that.

"First of all, not everyone who battles cancer loses hair, so this would not be relevant to many people," they told us. "And many people with cancer would be offended by this," they added.

We were disappointed. But as I've come to believe, everything happens for a reason.

About four months later, as the outlook for Mike's recovery was growing dim, I received a call from a man named Dana Ball. "I'm the executive director of the Iacocca Foundation," he told me. "Have you ever heard of Lee Iacocca?"

"Are you kidding?" I responded. In the 1980s Lee Iacocca was the equivalent of Steve Jobs or Bill Gates. As the CEO of Ford, he was credited with inventing the Mustang. As the CEO of Chrysler, he not only invented the minivan but turned the company around after negotiating a historic loan agreement with the US government—which he was able to pay back long before it was due. He was nothing less than an icon in the business world.

Now, in his retirement, Mr. Iacocca was focusing much of his energy on finding a cure for type 1 diabetes, the disease that had taken his wife's life. And the Iacocca Foundation was looking for an agency to help them share their story. Lee's daughter happened to see our sign on Newbury Street, around the corner from their offices, and suggested Dana give us a call.

Dana and I arranged to meet the next day to discuss the assignment in more detail and see if it was a good fit. Later that afternoon, I got a call from Dana. "Any chance you can fly to Nantucket next week to meet with Mr. Iacocca?" I couldn't believe it. I was going to meet Lee Iacocca. The first thing I did was call Mike. Although I admired Lee Iacocca, I've never been much of a car buff—but Mike was. He was over-the-top excited for us and gave me a short lesson on Lee Iacocca and his contributions to the auto industry to make sure I made a good impression. I also did my homework by reading Mr. Iacocca's most recent book on leadership.

As I sat with Mr. Iacocca, eating sandwiches and drinking iced tea on the patio of his Nantucket home, I had to remind myself it wasn't a dream. We talked for hours about everything—the foundation, our families, traveling, the auto industry, business, and leadership. But it was only later in the conversation, after he handed me a cigar and asked if I'd like to smoke with him, when the topic of Mike came up. I confided in him that the prognosis was not looking good and that I wanted to do something to keep Mike's fight alive—just as he was doing for his wife. I then shared the idea of having people wear a bald cap and told him how the organization had rejected it.

I don't remember the exact words he used, but after we each took a puff of our cigars, he looked at me as though he was my teacher and I was his student and said something to the effect of, "You need to be bold to make a difference, and that is a bold idea. You need to make it happen."

"He clearly liked you," Dana said to me on the flight home. "Mr. Iacocca doesn't smoke cigars with just anyone." For the entire flight home—and many days after—I couldn't get over my sense of excitement. Aside from the opportunity to work with Lee Iacocca, I knew how I could help Mike's fight continue.

Shortly after Mike passed, we put things in motion. We started a nonprofit organization called Small Army for a Cause and created the cancer fundraiser Be Bold, Be Bald! The entire agency poured their heart and soul into creating the event and making it happen. Interspersed with doing work for paying clients, often on nights and weekends, we worked together to attend to every detail, from creating the logo and website to procuring bald caps from China. We'd never managed an event like this before, but we were determined to make it a success.

The interesting thing is that, for the first time, we became our own client and had to tell our story. Without Mike. We told it exactly how we, as marketers, were trained to do it. We had our perfectly crafted positioning statement:

> *For people impacted by cancer, Be Bold, Be Bald! is a unique fundraising event to show solidarity with those who battle the disease while fighting with them. Unlike other cancer fundraisers, participants do not need to train or take time off from work to make an impact.*

We immediately began spreading the word on Facebook and other social channels, encouraging people to sign up for this great event. We specifically targeted people who were impacted by cancer and shared messages like these:

> *Go bald to honor those who fight cancer. No training or time off required.*

> *Go bald. Fight cancer. Get a free bald cap when you register.*

> *Go bald for just one day. Support those who battle cancer every day.*

We did everything by the book—but no one really seemed all that interested in that book. Yes, we got a few likes and comments here and there, and some people were registering. But this was a big, bold idea. It was different than anything else out there, and it had meaning. We didn't want a few people signing up for the event; we wanted thousands of people signing up for the event. It was personal.

We were devastated and could not understand why this was happening. In our heart of hearts, we believed this event was something everyone would want to be a part of. We had watched Mike fight his battle for over two years with enormous strength and courage. He may have looked weak, but he was stronger than any of us. We knew others had similar experiences, and this was an opportunity for everyone to recognize that unique strength and support the fight.

As we got closer to event, we became more devastated with the results and, one day, decided to do something a bit different. Rather than tell people about the event, we simply shared what was in our hearts.

One post simply read: *Bald is beautiful.*

Another simply shared what we had witnessed during Mike's battle: *True strength pushes vanity aside.*

We shared our soul. And suddenly, people began liking us—literally and figuratively. They shared our posts with their communities. In comments, people began sharing bald photos of themselves and loved ones who were battling the disease, confirming that bald is truly beautiful. They shared stories of the strength of loved ones who, like Mike, had battled so bravely. We were dumbfounded.

As these stories came in from people all over the world, we shared them. And with each story we shared, the community grew. They shared. They commented. They liked. They learned more. And they signed up. Today, we've raised more than $1 million for cancer charities, and tens of thousands of people have participated in our annual event.

When we shared from our heart instead of talking all about the event, people listened and acted. Not only that, they joined in and became a part of the story.

This experience caused us to take a step back and question everything we were taught as marketing professionals—the positioning statements, unique selling points, key messages, and so on. We studied hundreds of brands—ones we admired and felt loyalty toward as opposed to those with which we didn't quite feel as much of a connection. We sought to understand why we felt a stronger connection with some over others.

Instinct and marketing background would lead you to assume that certain products were simply superior to others. But when we were honest with ourselves, we admitted that the brands we loved most did not necessarily have superior products and services. They may have been better than a competitor's at one time or another, and some of the features may have been more important to us. But the reality was, many other options did virtually the same thing either equally well or better—and ultimately delivered the same benefit.

Harley-Davidson has a cult following, but their motorcycles are not really any better than BMW, Kawasaki, or Ducati. Apple's iPhone clearly started a revolution, but Samsung, Nokia, and others also have some amazing alternatives. North Face has great outdoor apparel, but so do Patagonia and Columbia. The same holds true for the coffee shop you prefer to patronize, the bar you most enjoy going to, the charity you give money to, and even the toilet paper you prefer to use. They do not necessarily have better products, but they are brands that, for some reason, you trust more, are proud to be associated with, and, in many cases, are willing to pay a premium for.

To discover what truly causes us to love the brands we love, we needed to look beyond what we were instinctually trained to believe.

We conducted dozens of conversations with marketing professionals, students, and general consumers and found that people have their own unique set of brands with which they feel a connection. However, when we looked deeper and asked why that connection exists, we found it has little to do with the products or services they offer. Of course, the products and services are good—but that was just the baseline requirement. The ante. For these brands, there was something much more meaningful.

With brands you love, you feel like you have a relationship with them. You are proud to be associated with them. The brands you love stand for something that is bigger than any product or service or unique differentiator. They have personalities that you are attracted to. They have beliefs that you share. And most of all, they have a story that you want to be a part of. They have a soul that you connect with.

As we looked back on our experience with Be Bold, Be Bald!, we realized that our initial storytelling attempt—the one we were trained to do as marketers—was a story no one wanted to hear. It was our elevator pitch. In that one chance we had in front of a potential participant, we rushed to sell them on what we did and how they could benefit from it. And we assumed that a great offer like a free bald cap would get them to move. But as people do with almost every sales pitch, they ignored it.

Yet when we shared from our soul, they opened theirs to us. We didn't try selling them anything. We didn't tell them why we were better than the other events or how easy we made it for them to raise money. And we didn't throw offers at them, trying to convince them to act quickly. In turn, those we connected with became more receptive about learning a bit more. They told their friends about us, visited our website, and registered to participate.

This is what loved brands do. They share their souls. When Apple launched the iPod—perhaps one of the most game-changing innovations of our time—they had ads that showed a silhouette of a person dancing with white headphones seamlessly connecting her ears to that small white device. That's it. For most brands, the instinct would have been to share the awesomeness of this invention—headlines touting the number of songs the device could hold, the unique aspects of the touch-sensitive interface, and the quality of sound. Instead, we see someone in sheer joy using this device. It wasn't a sales pitch. It was simply Apple sharing that they believed in a world of happiness and simplicity. We envisioned ourselves in that silhouette and immediately wanted to be in that world—that story. We sought out more information. We looked to the media, to our friends, to their website, and to retail stores to learn more. We bought iPods in droves, and our love for Apple got stronger.

Brands like Apple share their stories by carefully demonstrating what they believe as opposed to telling you what they do. They share their souls. This is how brands bring people into their stories. And once you are a part of the story, you want to know more.

On September 17, 2009, the first Be Bold, Be Bald! day arrived. I could barely sleep the night before and got out of bed at five o'clock in the morning in anticipation of the day ahead. I took a shower and quickly dried off so I could put the bald cap on my head. I carefully slipped the cap on, folding strands of hair sticking out under the edges, and stared at myself in the mirror. The latex caps were not quite what we had expected when they arrived from China. They were airtight, uncomfortable and, without a professional makeup artist to assist with proper application, made you look like a conehead from that 1980s *SNL* skit. We didn't have the time or budget to order other ones, and we just kept reminding ourselves, "This is not a physical challenge, it is a vanity challenge—one that many people going through cancer treatment do not have a choice about."

At seven o'clock in the morning, as I was getting ready to leave the house to do a bunch of radio and television interviews, my wife and kids came downstairs wearing their caps—even Josh, who was now almost two years old. They hugged me and told me how proud they were of what I was doing. The floodgates had been opened, and tears ran down my face—but these were not tears of sadness. They were tears of pride. I felt a sense of purpose and meaning unlike any other feeling I had experienced before.

As I shut the door behind me, I dried my eyes, posted a quick selfie to Facebook, and drove to my first interview. In the lobby of the television station, people sitting in the waiting area stared at me but quickly glanced away as soon as I caught their eyes. The receptionist avoided making any eye contact as she called the producer to let her know I had arrived. I felt uncomfortable and nervous—but I also felt confident as I got ready to open my soul to the public.

As the lights in the television studio beamed down on my latex-covered head, I could feel the pools of sweat building up under the bald cap and my eyes starting to pulse with pain. Then, the on-air light went on. The reporter sitting in the chair next to me introduced the segment, welcomed me to the show, and began, "So, Jeff, tell us why you decided to start this campaign." The pounding of my heart and cracking of my voice kept my tears at bay as I told her about Mike, our commitment to honoring those like him who bravely fight cancer, and raising money to help make a difference. As I opened my heart and shared my soul in each interview that morning, I felt more and more alive.

Although I hadn't slept much the night before and had gotten up at the crack of dawn, I was full of energy when I arrived at Small Army just before noon. I felt that same energy the moment I walked in the office and saw everyone wearing caps and sharing stories with one another—stories much like mine in the lobby of the television station. There was an aura at the agency that was larger than life itself. We were connected in a way we had never quite been before. It wasn't just because we all were wearing bald caps. We shared a common, meaningful purpose, and we were working together toward achieving it. Together, we were honoring Mike and other friends and loved ones who battled cancer by demonstrating that true strength pushes vanity aside.

We tried to go about the day as usual, but the energy and emotion could not be contained. An endless stream of e-mails and posts to the Be Bold, Be Bald! Facebook page came in from participants all over the world who were wearing bald caps and holding signs that shared who they were doing it for. Classes of elementary school children with their teachers. Families with loved ones who were currently battling cancer. Waitstaff at restaurants. Cancer survivors. And even a photo from a pilot in South Africa who was wearing his cap with a bunch of people in a local village. It was more rewarding than any check I'd ever received from a client.

In that first year, more than two thousand people across the country went bald to honor loved ones and got sponsored for their bold move. Together, they raised almost $150,000. We donated one hundred percent of the money to three different cancer charities—Dana Farber Cancer Institute, Livestrong, and the Leukemia and Lymphoma Foundation. And as draining as it had been to put together, we vowed to do it again the following year.

Mike's endless desire to give to organizations and help everyone who asked for it (and many who didn't) used to bother me. But I finally realized how good it felt to give, and I began to see why you do well when you do good. The local and national media attention we received in the weeks before, during, and after our inaugural event was more than we could ever have received for the work we did as an ad agency. Participants were sharing their experiences on social media and talking about Small Army and Be Bold, Be Bald! People who had never heard of Small Army suddenly knew our name. They had no idea what we did, but they knew who we were—an advertising agency that had started a nonprofit to raise money for cancer charities. At first, I thought, "If they don't know what we do or the quality of our work, it really won't matter." But I couldn't have been more wrong.

Small Army began to be viewed as the agency with a big heart. And I, the overemotional CEO, was recognized as the leader of this organization. I used to be embarrassed by my emotions. My family used to poke fun at me at weddings and other family events, just waiting for the waterworks to begin. My wife would make fun of me as I cried at sappy movies. But suddenly I became OK with it, because I realized it was part of who I was.

As we began sharing the Be Bold, Be Bald! story in new business meetings, potential clients saw more than our work. They saw our soul. They saw that we were an agency with a heart. We connected with people on a level much deeper than our capabilities and experience. Sure, our work had to be good. We had to have the experience the client needed, and we had to be priced on par with everyone else they met with. But that was just the baseline to be in the game. When virtually all else was equal—or even when the score was slightly out of our favor—we would come out on top. They liked us. They trusted us. And they wanted to be a part of our story.

You do not love a brand and want to be a part of its story because of what it does and how it does it. You do it because of *why* it does what it does. You do it because you share similar beliefs. You do it because you connect with its soul.

CHAPTER 4

MORAL

As I was lying in bed with my wife after a long day at work, my six-year-old daughter crawled in between us, anxious to tell us something.

"Daddy, you can't judge a book by its cover," she said to me.

I looked at her quizzically, having no idea what she was referring to but curious to understand what was on her mind. "What do you mean, Julia?"

"Well, like, if you were really ugly," she started with a short pause and giggle. I gave her a look of concern, letting her know this could be going in a bad direction. "Well, you're not ugly," she assured me. "But if you were, it wouldn't mean you're not nice."

"That's right, Julia," I agreed and then confirmed the important point. "And I'm not ugly, right?"

"You're not ugly, Dad. I was just giving an example. Our teacher read us a story in class today, and that was the moral."

I don't remember the details of the story she read in class that day, but I'll never forget how excited she was to share this lesson with me at the end of her day. It had meaning to her, and it stuck with her.

Every brand has a story that is evolving and being told every day. It is what you see, hear, taste, touch, and experience with the brand. Every purchase. Every visit. Every ad. Every interaction. Deep within that story, there is a soul. However, you can't define a soul. In fact, that is what makes a soul a soul. It is there, but you can't see it. You can feel it, but you can't touch it. And when you connect with it, you want to be a part of it. However, just like the story my daughter recalled from her kindergarten class, great stories have a moral. The moral is ultimately what gives the story its soul and creates the connection.

Consider the morals of some of the greatest stories we've ever read—ones that have been passed from generation to generation.

Pinocchio: Lying makes you look bad.
The Three Little Pigs: Hard work and dedication pay off.
Little Red Riding Hood: It's not safe to talk to strangers.

In each of these stories, and thousands of others like them, the moral is the core belief that guides the story. It gives reason for why things happen—why characters act the way they act, why there are consequences from those actions, and why the story ends the way it ends. Why did Pinocchio's nose grow every time he lied? Because lying makes you look bad. Why did the house of bricks withstand the wolf's huffing and puffing more than the houses of hay and sticks? Because hard work and dedication pay off. And why was the mean wolf in the bed instead of Grandma? Because it's not safe to talk to strangers. The moral is rarely directly stated or written in the text. It is embodied in the story itself. You may not recall every detail of the story, but as Julia did with the story she heard in school, you walk away with an understanding of the moral, and that is what stays with you.

The moral of a brand story is no different than the moral of any other tale. It is the core belief interpreted by the audience based on the story they hear and see. Sometimes, the moral is written in words or stated aloud. However, more often than not, it is the hidden undercurrent to the story and is inferred by the words, actions, and inactions of the brand and its representatives.

I often present the idea of a moral to groups of CEOs interested in building stronger relationships with their audiences. At the beginning of every presentation, I ask a simple question: "If your brand is a story, what is the moral?" Of course, in a room full of CEOs, answers are abundant. The hands quickly go up as they excitedly share their perspective.

At one recent group, the CEO of a meat-seasonings company proudly declared his brand's moral to be, "We are the region's leading provider of meat seasonings." The owner of an electrical contracting company said, "Service and commitment you can depend on." And the CEO of a supply chain logistics company explained that their moral was, "Your solution to the international supply chain management puzzle."

This group of CEOs responded no differently than other groups I had led. The responses are almost never true morals. More often than not, they share positioning statements, taglines, key messages, and product definitions.

The moral is not a statement about the brand. It is a belief—or truism of sorts—that is demonstrated by the brand and those who represent it. When we discover brands that share a belief that is meaningful to us, we feel a sense of connection with them. The stronger we hold the belief, the stronger our connection to the brand. We gravitate toward them as we would a friend. We trust them. When they mess up, we give them the benefit of the doubt. We introduce our friends to these brands. These are the brands that not only do well, they thrive in the good times and survive in the most turbulent of times. The brands that have the strongest relationships with people are those that convey a consistent and meaningful moral wherever and whenever their story is being told.

Consider Harley-Davidson, one of the most admired and loved brands in the world. In everything they do, they demonstrate that "freedom is exhilarating" (the moral of their story). This is why they make motorcycles that let you ride the open road. Motorcycles that let you be loud. Motorcycles that let you be you (custom bikes). It is the core belief that drives Harley-Davidson to do what they do every day.

Harley-Davidson does not necessarily state these words in their advertisements or communications materials. However, it is almost always implied. As a result, people who believe that "freedom is exhilarating" are attracted to Harley-Davidson. And the stronger you believe it, the stronger the attraction.

Disney believes it's fun to imagine. This is why they created theme parks that make you feel as if you've been taken into an entirely different world. This is why they create characters and movies that stretch the imagination. And it is why they create games and other experiences that encourage you to use your imagination. If you believe it's fun to imagine, you would likely love Disney. If you don't, then I would strongly advise against visiting a Disney park.

The brands we love most demonstrate their morals in virtually every aspect of their stories to every audience with which they build relationships. For Disney, this even includes calling their engineers "imagineers," reminding their workforce that it is fun to imagine.

Apple believes simple is better. You can see that in every aspect of the business. It starts with the name, Apple. It doesn't get much simpler than that. Even the logo is simply an apple with a small bite taken out of it. The packaging of each of their products has been designed to be as simple as possible—from the clean white box to the way the product is packaged and the directions are written. The user interfaces they create and continually evolve—from the original Mac to the Apple Watch—are designed with simplicity as their core philosophy. The stores have redefined the way retails stores are set up—simple, minimal, and clean. Apple oozes simplicity because they believe simple is better. And those who agree use Apple.

While the moral of the story is not a statement about the brand, it causes the audience to make assumptions about it. This virtue of a moral is especially important, as most people tend to be skeptical of claims made by brands. A good moral causes people to assume your strengths without you having to directly state them. In the case of Apple, the audience doesn't need to be told the product will be easy to set up or the user interface will be easy to use. We know Apple believes that simple is better and, therefore, assume these things.

Red Bull believes it takes energy to live life to the fullest. Their moral has nothing to do with the taste of the drink. In fact, many people who drink it would tell you it doesn't taste all that good. They drink Red Bull because it gives them energy.

The moral of the story recognizes that the brand is about something bigger than the individual products or services. Red Bull may be in the beverage industry, but they are really in the human-energy business. Most everything Red Bull does to promote their product is related to energy. Check out Red Bull's Instagram feed, and you'll find an endless stream of photos of people doing extreme activities—activities that clearly require energy—to enjoy life to the fullest. They even hold an annual event called Illume to encourage photographers to take photos and contribute to their gallery. They organize Flugtag events where competitors design and attempt to fly homemade flying machines off a cliff or pier. Everything they do is driven by the idea that it takes energy to live life to its fullest. The drink itself is often secondary, because they understand that people don't buy the drink because of the refreshing taste—they buy it and drink it because it gives them energy. Or, as their tagline states, "It gives you wings."

In the case of Red Bull, the moral comes to life in the tagline. Wings are their creative interpretation of energy. The moral of the story can inform everything the brand says and does—from the name and tagline to product development and partnerships.

Life is Good is the only brand I've found where the name of the brand is also the moral of the story. Life is Good believes life is good. While they started out as a t-shirt company, selling shirts on the street with a picture of a character named Jake and the words "Life is good," they have since expanded into a virtually endless line of products—all of which are associated with the good things in life. From t-shirts and mugs to pet products and Frisbees, if you believe life is good, you want to have one of their products. Beyond the products, the company has developed partnerships with brands like Hallmark: life is good, send a card. They've even created a Kids Foundation and Playmaker program where they bring optimism into the lives and classrooms of some of the most vulnerable kids. They believe life is good, and they are on a mission to help people have a good life.

The reality is that most brands do not share a consistent and meaningful moral. It is not that they don't possess that core belief, but rather that their core belief—and ultimately their soul—is being suffocated by marketing jargon, lack of focus, organizational changes, speed of business, or, in some cases, indifference.

In working with brands across countless industries and sizes, I've come to find that most every brand has a meaningful core belief. The brands we love most share it in every aspect of their businesses. However, for most others, that belief doesn't come to the surface as the moral of their story. In turn, the brand feels soulless, abandoned, or, in the case of most brands, confused. I'll elaborate.

Soulless Brands
In the spring of 2011, we were looking for new space for Small Army. Our lease on Newbury Street in Boston was coming to an end, and as people started to have to double up at workstations, it was time to expand into something larger.

While it was a time-consuming process to visit all the potential options, it was also interesting to see how different businesses designed and organized their spaces. For better or worse, every space seemed to have its own unique personality—the layout, the colors, the furniture, the flow of the space, the pictures on people's desks, the sounds of the office, the ways in which people were collaborating. Along our journey, we found ourselves in the bowels of a soulless brand. As we walked off the elevator, the fluorescent lights beamed down on the worn gray carpet. The white walls were empty aside from a few government-mandated posters regarding policies in the workplace. We listened to the hum of the cold air being pushed through vents as the people we walked by sat almost motionless in their cubicles working on their computers. The papers piled up next to them were just waiting to be read and processed. As we walked through the offices of this government agency, I almost expected to see the black dust of souls floating above people's heads. We thereafter referred to that option as "the soulless space." They were a soulless brand.

Soulless brands do not make any connections with people—and perhaps they have no interest in doing so. They are most often brands that either have virtually no competition or care only about making money, regardless of relationships. Government agencies and debt collectors often fall into this category. Rarely do you find a debt-collection agency that you feel a connection with. You know you've encountered one of these brands when you walk into their offices and feel absolutely nothing. However, herein lies the opportunity for many brands within this category.

Several years ago, I received a phone call from an executive at a debt-collection agency seeking help with telling their story. Unlike other debt-collection agencies that get paid a percentage of the funds recovered, this executive shared that they had a unique approach to this often-challenging problem for condominium associations trying to collect dues from delinquent tenants. Rather than charge hourly fees or a percentage of funds collected, they buy the debt from the condo association. In turn, the condo association gets guaranteed revenue, and the problem is taken off their hands. He also shared with me how they work with the delinquent tenants to understand their situations and help them identify possible ways to forgive or reduce the debt through government and other social programs. Of course, debt collection is not viewed as a glamorous business, and collectors are often seen as aggressive and unforgiving. However, I sensed that this group actually had a heart and was doing this for the right reasons, so we decided to help them discover their moral. After several weeks of discovery, we found their moral: "It's unfair to be punished for other people's problems." As you can imagine, this belief struck a nerve with condo-association boards who were suffering due to unpaid fees from tenants. And the more they expressed this belief, the more success they had.

Abandoned Souls

In my hometown of Newton, Massachusetts, there was this great local coffee shop I would often visit. If I had a meeting at the end of the day, I would stop by to grab a coffee and do some work before heading home to the craziness of the kids and the dog—where getting any work done was virtually impossible. The coffee wasn't necessarily artisanal, but it was good. The beans were ground with each order, and every latté was delivered with thoughtful milk froth art on the top (I'm always impressed with that extra touch). Every time I went in, I was welcomed with a smile, and after I ordered, they would bring my mocha and muffin over to the couch I had sunk into to do my work. Over the speakers, they played the coffeehouse station from XM at exactly the right volume, featuring acoustic folk artists. It was the perfect ambience to soothe my mind and help me think.

When the shop was purchased by another owner, everything changed except the name (the brand). The prices went up. They changed the type of coffee beans they used. They changed the music to a local radio station. I waited at the counter to get my coffee before I could sink into the couch. And the art on the top of my mocha disappeared. Some say that everything changed. I say that the brand abandoned its soul. The new owner thought he was buying a coffee shop and did everything he could to make it a bit more profitable. He changed to preground coffee. He replaced XM with the free local radio station, cut corners by hiring people who couldn't create milk-froth art, and made people wait in line to pick up their orders. What he didn't recognize was that he was buying a respite that happened to sell coffee. It was a coffee shop that believed "a comfortable escape can free our minds." And when the brand abandoned that belief, people stopped going. It is now a sushi restaurant.

This often happens when new leadership or ownership enters, believing they bought a product/service as opposed to a brand. It is possible to get back the soul, but you need to do it before it is too late and the sushi restaurant takes over.

Confused Souls

Years ago, I was working with a division of a Fortune-500 company that primarily grew through the acquisition of other companies. They recognized that, with all the growth, they had lost focus and were sharing an inconsistent story in the markets they served. As we began the process of discovering their moral, we interviewed dozens of people in different roles and positions across the organization. In speaking with executives at the top level of the organization, we learned about the strategy behind the acquisitions (past and future) and how each was intended to address a specific gap in their larger plan. However, as we went one or two levels deeper into the specific lines of business, we quickly noticed that these individuals were unaware of most anything that happened outside their line of work and had little understanding of the overall business strategy. They had no problem sharing what they did, who they did it for, and how they did it. But they all had very different interpretations of *why* they did what they did—especially now, as part of a larger organization. However, after several months of discovery, we identified a moral that clarified the story and brought everyone together.

In cases like this, it can require quite a bit of digging to find the moral. You need more than a few shovels—you may need an excavator. The founders of the organization are long gone. The leadership team who runs the organization joined years (or decades) after the company was founded and likely never asked why the company was started in the first place. The business model and strategies have completely shifted. The products have evolved, if not completely changed. And cultures are entirely different with each of these changes. But the moral is there if you look deep enough.

Most brands fall into this category. For a variety of reasons, including mergers and acquisitions, brands can seem a bit confused about who they are. Start-ups and newer brands often present themselves differently from minute to minute as they work to discover what appeals most to audiences. Entrepreneurial companies often change like chameleons, adjusting what they stand for based on current market conditions, competitive threats, or fads. And more established organizations with multiple audience segments present themselves differently, based on the unique demographics and needs of each audience. The more audiences they serve, the more faces they wear. I often refer to these brands as "Sybils." They have multiple personalities, and you are never quite sure which one you are going to get.

Of course, brands must actively evolve their business models, products, and services to stay competitive, reach new audiences, and build deeper relationships. However, the core belief that drives them to make these changes should be consistent. Otherwise, audiences will be confused by the story, and the brand's soul will feel confusing.

Time and time again, brand executives tell me there is no possible way they can find a core belief that is shared by every audience they serve. I've heard it all:

"I can't even get my leadership team to agree on anything."

"Our customers span multiple industries and continents. They don't even speak the same language."

"We don't even sell our products directly to the end users. The distributors are our customers, and their customers are our users."

"Our business customers have a completely different set of challenges and needs than our personal customers."

However, with each response, I need to remind them that the moral is not a key message or unique selling point. It is a belief. While every executive within an organization may have a unique perspective, and every audience segment may have a different need, I've always found that their hearts are all in the same place. And in the cases when they are not, the outlier is not a good fit for the brand. There have actually been times when, after presenting the moral of the story to an executive team, they all look at one another with slight grins on their faces, knowing exactly what the other person is thinking: "Well, that explains why [name of person/company] never quite worked out." He or she didn't believe in the moral. Their heart wasn't in the same place.

As we looked back at Be Bold, Be Bald!, we were able to pinpoint the moment our story took hold and we truly began building relationships with people. It was when we stopped approaching our story as an autobiography and, instead, started living our story and demonstrating the core belief that caused us to do what we did: "True strength pushes vanity aside." That was (and still is) the moral of our story. It is the belief that ultimately caused us to create the event. It is what we learned from Mike and what we wanted to share with others. People who shared this belief joined our story by responding to our posts and sharing their own personal experiences with us. Once we discovered the moral to our story and let it guide us, our story caught on and relationships flourished. Our moral gave us a soul that others connected with.

The reality is that a brand's core belief is often right in front of those who are leading it, but unless they take the time to discover it and look deep within to find it, they will not see it. When they do find it, they are likely to slap themselves across the forehead and say, "Of course!"—because that's what their soul has been telling them. But it will never be recognized as the moral of the story until they discover it and everyone who represents the brand lives by it.

Now it's time to learn how to discover the moral of your brand story.

SECTION TWO

Moral Discovery

CHAPTER 5

ALWAYS ASK WHY

My jaw was on the floor as my colleagues and I listened to the leaders of the nonprofit organization Beyond Conflict share stories about their peacekeeping work in places like South Africa, Kosovo, Northern Ireland, Cuba, and Bahrain. Since founding the organization more than twenty-five years earlier, Tim Phillips and his team had been working with world leaders to resolve major conflicts between countries, communities, religious groups, and others—moderating peace talks, driving policy changes, and building relationships among differing groups.

I could have listened to Tim share his stories for hours more—and, with his passion, he would have been happy to go on forever. But after about forty-five minutes, I needed to get to the heart of the matter. I sought desperately to understand what had caused this one person to create such a world-changing organization. As Tim stopped to take a breath in between stories, I jumped in and asked, "Why did you start doing all this?"

The conversation that followed went on for a while, and I cannot recall every word that was spoken. However, I'll never forget the way in which the story unfolded. It went something like this:

First, Tim sat back in his chair and paused for a minute. "It was a long time ago," he said as he closed his eyes and tried to take his

51

mind back in time. "It just kind of happened. I had an intuition to do something."

Yeah, right, I thought to myself. He just had an intuition of how he could bring peace to the world, and here we are. I looked at my colleagues in the room and knew they were thinking the same thing. Clearly, there was much more to the story here. So, I probed further: "Why did you have an intuition to do something?

Once again, Tim closed his eyes for a moment and then responded, "Well, I was working at a PR firm in Boston, helping one of our clients gain support to maintain a nuclear power plant in New Hampshire. I actually wasn't a big supporter of it, but it was my job," he said. "I ended up meeting with one of the leaders of the organization, who sat me down and gave me an in-depth lesson on the greenhouse effect." At this point, Tim gave us all a short lesson on the greenhouse effect. He then continued. "This was long before many people had ever heard of that, and I was immediately blown away. So, I decided to hold a seminar for journalists at Harvard's Kennedy School to teach others about it. That seminar led to an opportunity to participate in a summit in Rio in 1992. That was really the start of the organization. It was inspiring to see how these leaders from around the world, each with different backgrounds and cultures, could convene to help one another make a real difference."

OK. So this twenty-something kid from a PR firm learns something new and decides to hold a seminar at Harvard to get journalists to learn about it. Seems like something any normal person would do. Right? I couldn't help but ask, "Why did you decide to do the seminar?"

Everyone at the table was growing mesmerized by Tim's story. Even some of the people from his own team were beginning to hear a part of his past they had never heard before, and they waited with bated breath to learn more.

"Oh. Before the PR firm, I used to run fact-finding trips to Central America for policymakers and journalists. We would meet with political leaders in Central America to learn more about their cultures and political systems. I guess it really was that work that gave me the courage to do the seminar."

Now we're getting somewhere, I thought. "So, you used to organize fact-finding trips to Central America?" I asked. "Why did you do that?"

"Well, I was always into history. I felt like it gave me this kind of unconscious knowledge of the world. As a kid, I used to write letters to global leaders asking them to do things. So, I guess that's really where it all started."

"You wrote letters to global leaders? Why?"

"Well, because they are the ones who have the most power and influence to make a difference." And then it suddenly all came together. "That's really what we're doing at Beyond Conflict." Tim said. "We're using history to reconcile conflict. We don't go into these countries and just tell people what to do. We don't give seminars on conflict resolution and negotiation tactics. With every conflict, we begin by looking to history. We find places and people in the world who have experienced similar conflicts. Of course, no two conflicts are ever the exact same. But those who are in conflict respond much more positively to others who have been through similar experiences. Then we bring them together so they can listen and learn from one another. By bringing these people together, those who are experiencing the conflict can see themselves in those who have experienced similar conflicts elsewhere. They learn from them. They listen to them. And they begin to believe that they can do something to make things better."

It took a while to get there, but clearly the organization was founded on something much deeper than an intuition. There was a belief within Tim that actually went back to his childhood and was confirmed time and time again in his life. This dialogue became the foundation for the rest of the discussion that day and led us to the moral of their story.

Beyond Conflict isn't changing the world single-handedly. They are on a mission to give people facing conflict the courage to make a difference and move beyond their conflicts. They do what they do because they believe "we find our courage when we see ourselves in others." That is the moral of their story.

To find the moral of a brand story, you must start by looking deep within the brand itself and dig into its heart. That heart lives within the people who represent it. Brand leadership is always the best place to begin. You cannot truly get to the heart of the brand if you cannot speak with the people who ultimately guide it day in and day out—the founders, board members, CEO, and other C-level executives who drive the key business decisions and, most often, drive the overall culture of the business. Get them into a room together and find out what truly drives them and inspires them. And keep asking "Why?"

Toyota founder Sakichi Toyoda adopted a theory of "five why's," suggesting that, to get to the truest answer to a question, you need to ask "Why?" five times. This was especially helpful when it came to mechanics seeking to understand a problem. Here is the example that Wikipedia shares on this topic:

The vehicle will not start (the problem).

Why?—The battery is dead.

Why?—The alternator is not functioning.

Why?—The alternator belt has broken.

Why?—The alternator belt was well beyond its useful service life and not replaced.

Why?—The vehicle was not maintained according to the recommended service schedule.

As you try to get to the heart of an issue—especially among people who prefer to give short answers (unlike Tim)—this approach works very well. However, I've found that it doesn't always take five why's— and sometimes it takes more. It depends upon the initial question and the interviewee (some like to talk a lot, while others require a bit more probing). It is up to you to listen carefully and find the place or places where there is an opportunity to go deeper by asking why. And then the key is to keep asking it until you can't dig any further.

Interviewers often accept the initial response to a question as the final answer. However, if you leave it at that, you will not get very far. For example, most founders will give a similar reason for starting their companies:

"I was tired of working for someone else."

"I saw an opportunity to make more money."

Or, like Tim, "It was just an instinct."

But there is always a much deeper reason, and the answer is often very personal. In some cases, the story will go back to a childhood experience, a tragic event from their life or some other event that, until they are probed, they never even considered to be a reason they started their company—as it was so deep they didn't see it.

For this type of discussion, it is often most productive to get multiple people in a room together for a few hours. Reach into their hearts and let them build off one another's responses. In the conversation with Tim, other people on his team joined into the conversation and ended up sharing similar experiences of how a parent, friend, teacher, or even someone they saw on TV or read about in the news gave them the courage to make a difference in the world.

However, this approach can work only when the team works well together and is comfortable speaking openly and honestly with one another. These meetings are not intended to solve a problem or arrive at big decisions—those types of meetings can be highly contentious and argumentative. The sole purpose here is to understand why the brand does what it does—and, more specifically, understand why these people do what they do. The attendees must be comfortable sharing their souls and being open and honest with one another. If they all just follow what others say, then you might as well interview just one of them. For this reason, we often interview the CEO separately, to ensure he or she does not influence the opinions of others. (Sometimes CEOs also appreciate this special treatment.)

The leadership team is often the most critical and insightful for these conversations. However, the soul of the organization lies within all those who represent it—marketing and communications professionals, customer-service representatives, product managers, research and development professionals, sales professionals, and others. The more people you speak with, the better.

I remember a series of conversation with employees at Quincy Mutual Group, a 165-year-old insurance company just south of Boston, where the soul of the business came shining through in discussions with employees. Through discussions with their marketing professionals, insurance underwriters, claims processors, and others, one common theme kept coming through when we asked people why they joined the organization.

"My husband and I just had a baby, and I wanted to find a job that provided stability," one person shared.

"My previous company didn't seem to care much about the employees," another attendee stated with frustration. "People came and went all the time. I wanted to be in a place that I could stay, learn, and grow."

"I was laid off from my previous job and never wanted to experience that feeling of insecurity again," said one employee.

As we dug deeper and kept asking "why?" we discovered that almost every employee had a personal backstory about instability in their lives, and they each joined Quincy Mutual Group because of the stability it provided. The company was known not only for its financial stability, but also for giving its employees lifetime careers. They paid for 100 percent of employees' healthcare. They offered employees pensions. The majority of the people we spoke with had been at the company for at least ten years and had every intention of staying through to retirement. It is an insurance company full of people who deeply understand and care about a stable future.

While we spoke at length about the different types of insurance policies the company offered and the way they handled customer claims, the conversation inevitably went back to the same theme: stability. This was the most conservative company—and group of people—I had ever met. Every decision they made was carefully considered (including hiring us), with the ultimate determination based on how it would impact the future. This obsession with stability ran through the veins of everyone that was there. And it wasn't just about stability of the business. It was about the stability of relationships with partners, policyholders, and employees as well.

The claims team told stories of how each time they picked up the phone to help a policyholder with a claim, they would immediately enter the mindset of "how can I get them what they need?" as opposed to "how can I give them as little as possible?" (which was a perspective many of them said they had been taught in prior roles at other insurance companies). They understood that doing the right thing was right for business and right for the customers they served. The other option may have provided short-term gain for the company, but doing the right thing would ultimately provide long-term stability for the business and the relationship.

The underwriters who were responsible for drafting and issuing insurance policies shared similar perspectives. "We always try to work with the agents and their customers to provide the most comprehensive coverage," one underwriter told us. "And we would never try to sell them something they will never need. That would be unethical and eventually detrimental to everyone." Their comments were always framed around how their decisions and actions would impact the future.

The executives, perhaps the most conservative of all of them, took every measure to maintain the stability of the company, its employees, its policyholders, and its agents. They maintained a war chest of cash and investments in case disaster ever were to strike. They purchased reinsurance that further protected them from even the most unlikely of disasters—more than virtually any other insurance company ever buys. And they provided pensions, bonuses, and other benefits to employees to make sure they were always by their side.

Like every other insurance provider, Quincy Mutual sold insurance. But it was their obsession with providing stability to everyone who depended upon them that set them apart. Everything they did was based on the underlying belief (the moral of their story) that "our future depends on the choices we make today."

The "five why's" approach to getting to the heart of the matter is highly effective, especially when you start with the right questions. Rather than having a long list of questions and getting surface-level answers (which are often meaningless), focus on core questions and get deep responses. These five simple questions often get the most meaningful responses:

1. In less than one minute, how would you describe [brand X] to others unfamiliar with this industry?

Asking a brand representative to describe the brand in less than one minute can be like asking someone to sing the national anthem in thirty seconds. It is almost impossible to do. But this time limit forces them to try to be as clear and focused as they can be. In doing so, they highlight the one or two aspects they believe are most important. It's also important to clarify that the description is intended for someone outside the industry so they will stay away from buzzwords and industry jargon. By asking everyone this question, you get a broad understanding of how each person views the brand at its most basic level. And then you can continue the "five why's" approach to dig deeper. You will learn why the attributes they called out are important to them.

2. In your opinion, what is the mission of the organization?

Many brands have a mission statement. However, people rarely know what it is. In fact, many times people say, "Let me just pull up our website." That's not allowed. If you have to look it up, then you really don't live by it. This question helps you understand what the people representing the brand ultimately believe they are there for. (We'll talk more about the mission in the next chapter.)

3. Why did you start/join [brand]?

Whether it was a personal/family-related event or a situation with a former organization, or whether they just "needed a job" or they joined the company as an intern twenty years earlier, the backstory will tell you a lot about the organization. This was very apparent with Quincy Mutual Group and Beyond Conflict. This line of questioning can bring back many relevant memories. Let them go off on tangents—this is where the most unexpected insights and stories can come from. I never expected Tim to tell us about his childhood letters to world leaders, but that provided an interesting lens to the organization. The answer to this question often serves as the premise for the entire brand story.

4. What gets you most excited about coming to work each day?

The response to this question can help you understand the priorities of the organization from a more personal perspective. Often, these discussions start with high-level responses such as "I love helping customers solve their problems" or "I enjoy the collaborating with my colleagues." But you need to go much deeper than that. Why do they like helping customers solve problems? Ask for examples. Let them tell you stories. Remember that it can often take asking why four to five times and listening to several stories before understanding what really gets them excited.

5. What keeps you up at night?
Fear can be a highly emotional motivator. Remember that this process is intended to get to the heart. While this is often sparked by positive experiences, it can also be revealed through negative ones. Here, it is not only important to discover what causes leadership to worry, but why do those things cause so much angst?

These five simple questions can take hours to answer. Once the interviewees reach into their souls, they begin to share much more. No longer will you get surface-level responses and sound bites. You will begin to hear responses that are truly coming from the heart. When Tim began speaking about his childhood, he told me he had never even considered how that part of his life had impacted what he was doing today. They will laugh with you, cry with you, and share anger and frustration with you. These emotions are critical pieces of the response. Watch carefully to see when they get emotional—it is at those moments where their heart is truly beginning to show. You are right where you want to be.

Most teams do not take the time to share this information with one another. And as teams reveal their hearts and souls to one another, they bond and see one another in a more profound way. They understand one another's perspectives more, respect one another more, and, ultimately, work together better. Also, when the team is involved in the process, they feel invested in the outcome of the process. If they are not involved in the input, they will question the output. For this reason, it is critical that the leadership team, board, and other key stakeholders (especially the opinionated ones) are involved in the process. If they are not, you are setting yourself up for failure—or, at the very least, an unnecessarily long process.

As you interview the people, you will begin to identify consistent themes that motivate and drive them to do what they do. You will form several hypotheses about what the moral of the story may be. The words may not be perfectly formed, and the thoughts may still be spinning in your head, but the essence of the soul will begin to reveal itself. This is when you realize you are getting close to discovering the moral. However, do not jump to a conclusion too quickly. Form hypotheses and begin testing them. A brand has many beliefs, but only one lies at its core. Before you put a stake in the ground, you want to make sure the moral is the core belief for the brand. The following chapters will help make sure you do that.

CHAPTER 6
KNOW WHERE YOU'RE GOING

As someone who's always been intrigued by monkeys, I was excited to meet the team from Helping Hands: Monkey Helpers for the Disabled, Inc. and help them discover the moral of their story. As I prepared for the session, reviewing marketing materials and other information they sent over to us about the things monkeys can do for people living with disabilities, I felt I had a good sense of what the moral might be. But as I learned that day, it's not always obvious where the moral will lead you.

So, sitting around the conference room table, I confidently asked the members of the team why they joined the organization, what got them excited to be a part of it, and other discovery questions. In turn, they each talked about the magical relationship between monkeys and recipients. They talked about the painstaking efforts they take to ensure the match between the recipient and monkey helper is the best possible. And they spoke at length about the benefits of opposable thumbs and great mobility, whereby monkeys could be much more helpful than other service animals. On command, they can retrieve a bottle of water, deliver it to the recipient, unscrew the cap, and insert a straw so the recipient can drink. They can fetch the TV remote, adjust the volume, and change channels. They can pick up the phone for recipients when they get a call. When trained properly (which requires significant time, resources, and patience), these service animals can do almost anything a human can do. But as we kept asking why, we discovered something much more meaningful.

The reality was that, aside from the monkey, the recipients still had a full-time aide or caretaker who was with them twenty-four hours a day, seven days a week and was capable of doing anything a monkey could do. So, with this in mind, we asked, "Why do they really need or want a monkey?"

One person said she often heard the recipients say that "the monkey is the reason I get up every morning." Another quoted a recipient who recently said, "The monkey gives me a reason to live." And another team member quoted a recipient who said, "The monkey makes me feel better about myself." None of the recipients were talking about all the things the monkeys physically did for them. They didn't talk about the remote-control use or phone retrieval or water delivery. And with one more why, the conversation revealed what mattered most.

From the moment they are injured or diagnosed, this audience depends upon others to take care of them—family members, friends, neighbors, and professional caretakers responsible for doing the most basic activities. Getting them food. Changing the TV channel. Holding the phone. Changing their clothes. Tying their shoes. These individuals are completely dependent upon others to live. And this complete dependency on others causes them to feel useless and frustrated—especially when the caretaker is a friend or family member.

As the conversation moved in this direction, my mind wandered for a bit as I started to think about my own parents. I had visions of my sixty-five-year-old mother sitting almost motionless in her wheelchair. She was desperately trying to keep from spilling the hot tea as her trembling hands brought the mug to her mouth. Then, as some of the tea entered her mouth and some fell onto her lap, tears came to her eyes, and she yelled at my father for making the tea too hot and putting in too much honey. My father, feeling completely unappreciated, screamed back in frustration, as he was just trying his best to help.

But my mother's frustration wasn't truly with my father. Years ago, as her multiple sclerosis advanced and she lost feeling and mobility in her limbs, she grew frustrated with her inability to do anything on her own. She appreciated my father for helping her but also felt an unhealthy dependency upon him. There was lots of resentment between them. It pained my mother to not be able to do the things she loved—like dancing and hosting parties. But perhaps even more frustrating was her inability to do the simple things like get a cup of tea for herself or even just get dressed on her own.

And the resentment went both ways. My dad, who became a full-time caretaker in retirement, was held back from the things he would love to do, like travel or go to parties with friends. While they stayed married until the day my mother passed away, the relationship was anything but healthy. I immediately began to see the promise of monkey helpers.

We learned that, much like humans, monkeys thrive on helping others. But they also very much depend upon others to help them. For a person living with a disability, having a service monkey wasn't about having another person (or animal) to take care of them. It was quite the opposite. With a monkey helper, these people who were otherwise dependent upon everyone else now had someone that depended upon them. It made them feel wanted. And it gave them a reason to live. The monkey made them feel more alive.

Once we recognized that the goal of the service monkey—and the organization—wasn't about having another caretaker but was rather about helping disabled individuals feel more alive, we were able to discover the moral of the story: "You feel more alive when you feel needed."

Many successful authors will tell you that, before they begin writing a book, they know how it is going to end. By taking this approach, the writers have something to work toward. Regardless of how much characters evolve, situations change, and drama occurs, the writers can always write to the end goal they have in mind. Even when the path changes or hurdles jump in the way, there's a beacon they can see from wherever they are and can always head toward it.

Brands need that beacon too. The moral of your story serves as the compass for your brand. It is that core belief that guides it to do what it does. But ultimately, your compass needs to get your brand to where it wants to go, so that destination must be understood and clearly defined in order to be certain that your moral will get you there. I call that destination the "happily-ever-after." A strong moral guides a brand to its happily-ever-after. In Monkey Helpers' happily-ever-after, people with disabilities feel more alive. And once we identified that, we were able to discover their moral.

Many brand executives will tell you they have this destination and refer to it as their mission. However, few people actually remember what their mission is. And more often than not, mission statements tend to be self-serving, inward-facing statements that are more about brand success than customer success.

Consider these examples of published mission statements from Fortune 500 companies (who are not among the most admired brands):

> *Brand #1: To achieve profitable growth through superior customer service, innovation, quality and commitment.*

> *Brand #2: To be the best in the eyes of our customers, employees and shareholders.*

> *Brand 3: To build shareholder value by delivering pharmaceutical and healthcare products, services and solutions in innovative and cost effective ways.*

Brand #4: To be the global energy company most admired for its people, partnership and performance.

Brand #5: To be the leader in every market we serve, to the benefit of our customers and our shareholders.

Brands often write mission statements as though they were crafting their personal goals. They are about revenue, market share, profitability, shareholder value, and other inward-facing goals. From an internal organizational perspective, these statements can be very valuable. They do provide goals for everyone within the organization to strive toward. And in some cases, these statements remind them what they need to do to get there. So don't rush to throw away your mission statement—but don't force it to be the beacon for your story.

Companies that have these types of mission statements experience considerable challenges in building relationships with people. And they often lead to unattractive morals. If profitability, market share, and domination are the happily-ever-afters your brand is taking people to, you will surely lose a lot of people along the way, and many will have little interest in joining you in the first place. These missions are exactly the kind of statements that cause consumers to be skeptical about every pitch a brand makes to them. They are sending a clear message that the brand is in it for themselves. Unless consumers are convinced otherwise, they assume the money they pay for products and services is going toward self-serving causes like executive bonuses, corporate boondoggles, and other things that have zero benefit to them. Their "philanthropic" deeds are viewed as marketing ploys. And ultimately consumers struggle to accept the value of the brand's products and services. These are the brands we feel the least passionate about.

Your moral needs to guide you to a destination that everyone involved in your story will want to be a part of—executives, employees, shareholders, customers, partners, donors, and others. They need to believe your brand has a purpose bigger than profit and domination.

Nonprofits, by definition, have this perspective. They were founded with goals much more aspirational and altruistic than making profit or being better than everyone else. Their idea of shareholder return has a much greater reward, and it often comes from a very deep belief in a cause. They have goals of making a difference in something bigger than themselves. Mothers Against Drunk Driving wants a world with fewer accidents from drunk driving. The American Red Cross wants a world with less suffering. Inner-city organizations want to see communities with less violence, more opportunities for youth, and better health for all. Beyond Conflict wants a world where people have the courage to make a difference.

These are stories we all want to be a part of. This is one of the reasons we feel a much closer bond with nonprofit brands than for-profit brands. We happily give our time and money to them without getting any product or service in return. We do so because we feel strongly about where they are taking their stories and believe that, with our support, they can get there.

For a brand to discover its moral, it must define its happily-ever-after—the destination that everyone in its story would be excited to be a part of and can rally around.

It should come as no surprise that, when we studied the world's most admired brands, we found many of them already think in this perspective. Nike says it wants to "bring inspiration and innovation to every athlete in the world." Starbucks wants to "inspire and nurture the human spirit." Alphabet (Google) is looking "to organize the world's information." And Amazon wants to be "Earth's most customer-centric company, where customers can find and discover anything."

Each of these organizations has a happily-ever-after that everyone can rally around. Each views its role as one that contributes positively to the world and has a clear focus on getting there. These are the brands we fall in love with.

Of course, not all happily-ever-afters need to be so lofty.

Swissbäkers is a small restaurant chain in Boston, serving authentic Swiss bakery goods, sandwiches, and coffee. While CEO and head baker Thomas Stohr was giving me a tour of their commissary, I was indulging in the sweet smell of fresh croissants, Swiss pretzels, and chocolate pastries. As I mentally enjoyed the feast, Thomas explained all the differences between Swiss pastries and more common American pastries. "A Swiss Berliner has less than half the calories of an American donut," he proudly stated.

When we walked by the young baker rolling pretzels, Thomas was quick to point out, "Every pretzel goes through this lye machine, which is kind of like an intense salt car wash." He further warned, "Lye is an incredibly strong ingredient that must be handled very carefully in the baking process. That's why the pretzels you get in the mall don't have it, but that's what really makes a Swiss pretzel a Swiss pretzel. It's one of the only lye machines in all of the United States."

As Thomas's wife and business partner, Helene, was meticulously preparing the pastries, he carefully picked up a finished tray of cookies and tarts. Each treat was a demonstration of perfection: cookies with perfectly shaped hearts of strawberry filling, surrounded by a dusting of white powdered sugar. Tarts with beautiful weaves of crust covering the creamy filling, and freshly cut fruit carefully placed on top it all. The pastries were all neatly laid out on a clean tray, covered, and wrapped with a bow and ready to go out to a customer. "It's not just about the taste of the food. It needs to look as good as it tastes," he commented.

As we walked from the commissary toward the front of the house, where customers were being served, we stopped in front of two swinging doors and a mirror, where there was a mannequin dressed in the Swissbäkers uniform. "This is Armando," Thomas said, as though introducing me to one of his staff. "He is a food-loving guest hugger," he said is his strong Swiss accent. "He's here to remind everyone what they should look like and how they should behave with customers when they walk through these doors. We are all food-loving guest huggers here."

After the tour, we grabbed a few lattés and sat down with Helene and their two sons, who were also involved in the business. I couldn't help but dig a bit deeper on the "food-loving people huggers" comment that Thomas made a few moments earlier. It didn't take long before Helene and Thomas were sharing stories of their life in Switzerland. "There was just this feeling you have when you are there. The food. The love. The people. The appreciation of every moment. That is what we want people to feel when they are here."

In that moment, we discovered their happily-ever-after. The food was simply the means to a much more meaningful end. Whether customers were eating in their store, grabbing a pastry to go, or enjoying their food at a catered event, the happily-ever-after was people experiencing that feeling of being Swiss for a moment. It was about the experience. Helene and Thomas definitely have goals of opening more restaurants, increasing profitability, and providing great customer service. But their happily-ever-after— the one thing they want everyone in their story to experience—is simple. They want people to have the feeling Helene and Thomas fondly remember from their lives in Switzerland. Driving them to that destination is the single core belief that "every moment counts" (the moral of their story). And I was definitely feeling it that day.

Brands that are most successful in building relationships with people have a happily-ever-after that appeals to everyone in their story. It is often what caused them to exist in the first place. For Helene and Thomas, they literally wanted their customers to get a taste of what it felt like to be back in their home country. However, many businesses quickly lose sight of their destination. They see only what is right in front of them. They focus on revenue goals, sales quotas, fundraising, inventory requirements, supply needs, competitive threats, partnerships, and product innovation. The people who started the business move on. Investors take over. And they lose sight of their true destination.

Whether it be a for-profit or not-for-profit, every brand needs to have a clear view of its happily-ever-after. Without it, they cannot be sure their moral will guide them where they want to go. A brand's happily-ever-after is ultimately its reason for being. It must be simple. And it must be something that everyone who represents it, and everyone who considers being a part of it, can easily understand and connect with.

When considering your happily-ever-after, remember these important criteria:

1. Everyone in your story will want to go there.
One of the most common mistakes brands make is thinking their brand story is all about them. They have grand visions related to profitability, market share, competitive advantage, and revenue growth. Or, in some cases, they take it to an even grander level of being the "most trusted" or "most admired" brand in their industry. These goals may be lofty and aspirational to all those who work there or have a stake in the business, but most consumers don't care much about that destination. That's not a happily-ever-after that most would want to be a part of—and many could even be turned off by it. The Fortune 500 brands noted earlier are clear examples of this. When considering a happily-ever-after, brands need to look beyond their products and services and consider what happens when people engage with them. For Thomas and Helene, they just wanted people to feel good—that same feeling they knew and loved when they were in their homeland. Sounds like a place I'd like to go.

2. It is reasonably achievable to get there.
Your happily-ever-after must be achievable in the eyes of all who
are part of your story, and they need to believe you can get there
while you are together. Your audience wants to reach happily-ever-after over and over again. Swissbäkers wasn't taking people to
Switzerland—that's probably more achievable for an airline than
it is for a bakery. If they promised Switzerland, we wouldn't believe
it—and we would either be less apt to go in the first place or disappointed when we didn't get there. They simply wanted people to
experience the good feeling you get when you are there. While the
Red Cross may dream of a world without suffering, their happily-
ever-after is a world with less of it. This is much more attainable
and, as a result, something that we can much more comfortably
support.

3. It's a place we can all keep going back to.
Your happily-ever-after must be reachable time and time again.
If it has a finite, one-time ending, your brand will find itself out
of business when it gets there. For Swissbäkers, you can experience that Swiss feeling every time you go there. If once you felt it
you could not feel it again, that would not be good for business.
Perhaps a better example is a cancer foundation that defines
their happily-ever-after as a world without cancer. The organization would put themselves out of business once they get there,
because the journey would be over. Of course, this may be OK
for a nonprofit with a finite goal. But for most brands, going out
of business is not really a happily-ever-after that everyone wants
to achieve.

4. It is clear and simple.
There is no need to make your happily-ever-after any more com-
plicated than it needs to be. It does not need to explain how you
are going to get there. How you are going to get there will likely

change over time. Today, Swissbäkers serves chocolate, pastries, pretzels, and sandwiches in restaurants. Tomorrow, they may expand their offerings, establish new methods of distribution, and develop additional partnerships. But their happily-ever-after will serve as their beacon, and their moral will guide them there.

Your brand's happily-ever-after reminds everyone where you are going. It is your reason for being. In some cases, your happily-ever-after may differentiate you from your competition, but that is not the intent of it. For some brands, it will differentiate them because competitors haven't articulated one at all. In other cases, competitors will have come to believe that their self-serving missions are their happily-ever-afters—and few people are interested in going there. Differentiation may be a benefit of a happily-ever-after, but it is not a requirement. Many brands share the same destination. The difference between each brand is how you will get there—and that is driven by the moral of the story.

Swissbäkers wants you to feel that feeling they get when they are in Switzerland. In Switzerland, every train arrives exactly on schedule. Every watch is made with the greatest precision. And you'll rarely see a Swiss person arrive late to a meeting. True to the core of who they are, Swissbäkers believes "every moment counts." Every moment a customer is sitting in one of their restaurants, waiting in line for a coffee, eating a pretzel in a car, or enjoying food at an event, they want every moment to be a great one. They also know the importance of every moment they put into everything they do: carefully putting each pretzel though the lye machine, baking each loaf of bread for the exact amount of time, meticulously placing each pastry on the tray, wrapping the bow perfectly around the platter, wearing the uniform just right (like Armando does), and always feeling like every customer is getting a hug when they are with you. Swissbäkers is about more than the food. At Swissbäkers, they want you to feel that good Swiss feeling. And when you believe that every moment counts, you are likely to make that happen for everyone around you.

Only when you know where you need to go can you discover the moral that can guide you there.

CHAPTER 7

LOOK DEEPER THAN DEMOGRAPHICS

S tanding in front of a group of executives at Boston Medical Center (BMC), I explained, "The moral of the story is a belief that is not only true to you, but one that you also share with your audience."

"Wait a second. You expect to find one belief that all of our audiences share? Doctors, nurses, patients, and donors?" one executive asked with disbelief.

"Exactly," I confidently replied.

"That's impossible," he challenged. "Our patients and donors are two completely different sets of people. Our patients are primarily low-income African American, Hispanic, Latino, and Asian people living in the most vulnerable communities in Boston," he explained. "And our donors are wealthy people living in the suburbs. The two audiences are nothing alike."

"That's true," I replied. (I always find it best to agree with someone before beginning this common debate.) "Your audiences may not look the same, live in the same neighborhoods, or share the same demographics. But that doesn't mean they do not share similar beliefs," I told him. "In fact, the way in which they express their beliefs may be different as well. But deep down, I'm confident there is a common belief that is shared among all your audiences. And we will find it."

With that challenge, we set out to find the moral of the story for Boston Medical Center.

Unlike most of the other world-renowned hospitals in Boston, BMC caters primarily to those who live in the inner city. The patient population is heavily made up of racially diverse, lower-income people who live in areas most vulnerable to disease and illness. Poor living conditions, violence, drugs, and other factors have a considerable impact on the health and well-being of the patient population.

"More than thirty-five percent of our patients don't show up for primary-care appointments, and more than thirty percent of women diagnosed with cancer don't show up for their follow-up appointments," one administrator shared with us. "They can't afford the cost of the bus, a babysitter, or a day off from work to get here."

Due to the population BMC serves, the majority of patients are on state or federally subsidized health insurance programs that often pay less than half of what commercial insurers may pay for the same exact procedure. As a result, BMC depends greatly on government grants and major philanthropic contributions from wealthy individuals who generally live in more affluent suburbs of the city and go elsewhere for their medical care.

From the moment we began speaking with people within BMC, it was clear this was an organization that truly cared about their patients and believed in their mission to "provide exceptional care without exception." As we used the "five why's" approach to dig deeper, we found many of them had their own heartfelt stories as to why that mission was so important to them.

"Working with this population is so much more rewarding," one physician told us. "I feel like I'm really making a difference in the world."

"This was my family's hospital," a nurse shared. "I was always inspired by how much this place cared about us. It was always my dream to work here."

The administrators at the organization would speak in awe about the nurses and physicians, who often go above and beyond their call of duty to take care of their patients.

"The doctors and nurses care so much about their patients," we were told time and time again. "They go out of their way to create programs like the food pantry and often volunteer their time to make them happen."

"The physicians who work at BMC are some of the most talented, caring, and giving people in the world," administrators would tell us. "They could work anywhere—and get paid more doing it—but they choose to work here."

And when we spoke with the development professionals, they would go on about their donors who give so much money to the hospital to take care of this vulnerable population.

"Our donors are the most generous people," the development officers repeatedly told us. "They really care for the people in Boston. Without them, we would not be able to do what we do."

It was clear that everyone who worked at BMC felt honored to work there and did what they could to take care of patients. Many even volunteered outside the scope of their jobs to support some of BMC's many free patient programs, and the donors showed their support with generous financial contributions. But what about the patients? What belief did they share with the employees and donors?

While we were conducting our internal interviews, I remember sitting with the chief of family medicine in his office. During our conversation, I was distracted by a large framed letter hanging on his wall that was written by a child. The letter, which I took a photo of, read:

> "Hi Doctor. I can't wait to see you to say thank you for all your help you done for me and my family. I'm in second grade now and one day I will be in college. I study to be a doctor like you and I want to help you when you can't walk anymore. I want you to be my patient because you are my best doctor ever for my family. Thank you."

I couldn't help but ask about this note, and as the chief shared the story of this patient, his face lit up with pride. "That's why I love what I do," he shared. "Our patients are the most grateful patients in the world. They have huge hearts."

Throughout the time we were interviewing people within BMC, I also became friendly with Kathy, the woman at the front desk in the fundraising office. Kathy told me they received kind notes from patients all the time and shared some with me. Many of the notes were similar to the one hanging on the chief's wall, and some referenced a small amount of money, one dollar or five dollars, that they included in the envelope. "I wish I had more to give, but I hope that this can help."

In the office of one of the development team members, I spotted a bright-pink afghan sitting on a chair. When I asked who made it, he told me it was a gift from a patient and continued to tell of the many handmade gifts they receive from the patients they care for—beautiful drawings and paintings, kind handwritten notes, pictures of families, and other random gifts from people's homes.

We began looking at the patients from a different perspective. We thought about the statistics of patients missing appointments and realized there was a much deeper reason for it. They wouldn't miss a day of work, because they needed to put food on their family's table. They wouldn't leave children at home alone, because it was their responsibility to take care of them. And they wouldn't spend money on the bus or a babysitter, because it would be better spent on rent or food for their family. They cared so deeply about everyone around them that they often put themselves second. The kind notes, gifts, and money they were giving to the hospital were another demonstration of this population's depth of care and generosity.

As we went out into the communities, we held on to this perspective. We met and spoke with so many loving people. They cared deeply about their families, with three and sometimes even four generations of a family living together in the same home. The health and happiness of their family and friends were far more important than money and prestige. They shared endless stories of helping one another with schoolwork, groceries, and rides to appointments and providing food and shelter to those in need. This community may have had little to give, but they gave so much.

As we were putting together our thoughts for the moral of the story, we came across a YouTube video that shows a young man asking patrons in a pizza shop for a slice of pizza. One by one, he goes up to each of them, tells them he is hungry and doesn't have any money, and asks if he can have a slice. But as they all chow down their pizza, they reject his request. A while later, the video shows a friend of the young man giving a whole pizza to a homeless man on the street. As the homeless man eats his pizza, the young man who had previously approached the pizza-shop patrons walks up to him, tells him he is hungry, and asks for a slice. Without hesitation, the homeless man gives the young man a slice of pizza. Those who have the least often give the most. Each time I watch this video, I cry.

I'll never forget presenting the moral of the BMC story to the CEO, CFO, and marketing executives of the organization. We walked into the room, confident we had found a moral that was true to every one of their audiences and could ultimately help them build relationships. We walked them through our research and, shortly before presenting the moral, shared the video of the young man and the pizza.

Then we watched as they each shed a tear when we shared the moral of the story: "Life's greatest privilege is taking care of those around you."

First and foremost, this belief clearly guided the soul of everyone who worked at BMC. The doctors, nurses, administrators, and staff felt privileged to work there and help those they served. It guided donors who gave substantial funding to help BMC take care of those who live around them. And perhaps more than anyone else, this belief rang true to those who went to BMC for medical care. BMC serves people who believe that life's greatest privilege is taking care of those around them. That's why they put family over career. That's why they choose to stay home with a child instead of going to their checkup. And it's why they give whatever they can to help those who help them.

Like BMC, most brands seek to build relationships with audiences that seem nothing alike from a demographic perspective. They have business customers that seem completely different from nonbusiness customers. Customers within one industry have a completely different set of needs than those in other industries. And visitors who visit one store location seem nothing like the patrons of another one. The audiences look different, but when it comes to a relationship with your brand, their hearts are in the same place.

Brands often think of their audiences in terms of demographics. They target Hispanic women between the ages of twenty-five and fifty-four with household incomes of $50,000 or more. They seek to reach IT (information technology) executives at health-care organizations with revenues of more than $100 million. They target parents of kids between the ages of three and fifteen who live within a ten-mile radius of their store location. This can be an effective way to look at your audience, as it helps to put some parameters around your target and gives you a general understanding of who they are. However, this quantitative approach also causes brands to believe that their audiences are more different than they really are.

As the BMC story demonstrates, the donor and patient audiences look almost nothing alike from a demographic perspective. Donors are predominantly white, while the patients are much more ethnically diverse. Most major donors have household incomes of more than $250,000, while most patients have incomes of less than $40,000. And most donors live in suburban communities, while most patients live in urban ones. From a media targeting perspective, this is helpful information, as BMC would want to place their media message in channels that best reached these segments. However, from a messaging and communications perspective, it was important to recognize that everyone they sought to build relationships with had one thing in common: they believe that life's greatest privilege is taking care of those around you.

When you overlay your demographic profile with the moral, you gain a much more meaningful and actionable profile of your entire audience. In some cases, the moral can broaden your perspective beyond the typical demographic. And in other cases, it can exclude others within the demographic segment you have defined.

For BMC, the moral caused us to market beyond inner-city communities, where the traditional demographic lived, into other nearby communities where people who likely shared our moral lived. As a result, BMC not only attracted many new patients, but those patients were also using commercial healthcare plans that often paid more than the subsidized plans.

It is important to remember that, first and foremost, the moral of the story is the core belief that defines why the organization does what it does. A brand should not define their moral based on what an audience believes. Instead, they must first discover what they believe and then identify how the audience shares that with them. Otherwise, the brand will end up trying to be something they are not—and that is not often a recipe for success. I remember a female friend excitedly telling me about a guy she had met. He loved the outdoors, so she had been going camping with him almost every weekend. The only problem was that she hated the outdoors and was miserable camping—but she wanted him to like her so much that she tried to make him believe otherwise. That relationship didn't last long. The same will happen for brands who take that approach.

The most effective way to determine if and how your audiences live by your moral is to speak with them directly. Call them on the phone. Stop them in the streets. Reach out to them on e-mail. Conduct a focus group. The point is to talk with them. And most important, look beyond the surface and apply the rule of five why's. Test hypotheses that you may have identified from internal discovery and see how they respond. Everyone acts upon their beliefs in a different way. Understanding how each audience acts on the belief is a critical part of building the relationship with them. When you understand how the brand's belief applies to their lives, you will be able to connect and build stronger relationships with them.

At BMC, the belief is what caused the doctors and nurses to work at the hospital. For donors, it is what caused them to support the hospital—and many other community organizations. And for patients, it is what caused them to care so deeply about their family and community.

With a moral that is shared among everyone, your brand does not need to try and be something different for each audience. The specific messages and calls to action may be unique, but the heart and soul remain the same. As we worked with BMC to drive potential patients to book primary-care appointments, we shared photos of real families in the communities, with lines that promoted the belief that we all help one another. "Taking care of those around us helps us all." Or "The health of all of us depends on each and every one of us." These ads were meticulously placed where people within the primary patient markets would see them. In a parallel effort, a campaign invited potential donors to hear stories from some of the people BMC has helped. Wayne, a young black man, shared his story of battling stage 4 cancer. Cassie, a heroin addict, shared how BMC helped her get back on her feet and reunite with her children. And Jeff, a Boston Marathon attack survivor, shared how BMC saved his life. While both campaigns had different messages and calls to action, they both shared the belief that "life's greatest privilege is taking care of those around you." And both campaigns shared the tagline "Stronger Together."

The moral of your story enables you to more effectively pinpoint your audience, because it is the shared belief that causes you to connect with them. If someone believes in the moral, then he or she could be a customer. However, perhaps more important is the opposite—if someone does not believe in the moral of your story, than he or she would not be a good customer.

Life is Good believes "life is good." If you believe that life is good, you will likely want to be involved in their story. (My kids often make fun of my large collection of Life is Good apparel.) However, if you don't believe Life is Good, you are probably not a candidate for their products. In this case, I'd recommend the brand Life is Crap.

Similarly, people who do not believe that "life's greatest privilege is taking care of those around you" will likely choose the elite Boston hospitals over BMC. And that's OK. BMC does not need to waste time or money communicating with this audience; no matter how hard they try, those people will almost never choose BMC over the others.

The beauty of a moral is that you do not need to sell it to your audience. Ultimately, everyone falls into one of three categories:

1. Believers: Those who agree with your moral
2. Nonbelievers: Those who don't agree with your moral
3. Undecided: Those who don't disagree with your moral

The believers are your most attainable customers. If they share your belief, then they will be open to a relationship with you. The nonbelievers are your least likely customers. They may look perfect from a demographic profile perspective, but if they do not share your belief, you are fighting a huge uphill battle to build a relationship with them. You can try hard to sell them your wares, but ultimately, it will not be a good fit. And then there are the undecideds—those who don't disagree. This group is open to your belief, but they really haven't thought much about it. They don't necessarily want it or need to be sold on it, but they could use some education to help get them there or some awareness to cause them to think about it.

Brands are most successful when there are many believers, and they focus on that audience. There is opportunity with the undecided, and brands can do some work to shift them into believers by educating them. However, one of the most lethal things a brand can do is try to convert nonbelievers to believers. It is an arduous battle that is almost impossible to win and can destroy a brand. Brands must be able to recognize when they are speaking with nonbelievers and quickly move on.

In the world of advertising, acquiring new business can often be a long and grueling process. Potential clients send requests for proposals to multiple agencies, asking for pages and pages of information. If you are fortunate enough to make it through the first cut and get invited to continue to the next round, you are then often required to complete an assignment—without pay—and present it to the review team. These assignments can often demand hundreds of hours of resources and considerable out-of-pocket expenses, and they demand strategic thinking, research, creative ideas, and some implementation of those ideas into videos or other elements. These pitches can also cause considerable stress and financial drain on agencies as resources that are typically working on paid client work get diverted to these massive competitive reviews. The agency is then required to either force everyone to work nonstop to get through these times or pay freelancers to pick up the slack.

With this process, it is critical that we participate only in the pitches we believe we have a strong chance of winning. Otherwise, we risk wasting considerable time and resources—and, perhaps even worse, negatively impacting the relationships we have developed with existing clients.

At Small Army, our moral guides us in these situations. We believe the strongest relationships are built upon shared beliefs. Therefore, before proceeding with any new business endeavor, we try to determine if the potential client shares that belief. If we believe they don't, we politely pass on the request for proposal (RFP)—and save ourselves considerable time and aggravation. If we believe they do, we move forward, but also continually watch for any indication that they are nonbelievers.

Of course, the RFP will never make mention of this statement. However, we can clearly see when the belief does or doesn't exist. For example, if the timeline or process in the RFP does not allow for the agency to meet with the client before the assignment needs to be done, we will pass. This is a clear sign that they do not believe in building relationships or care much about shared beliefs, as they have no interest in being collaborative and helping us understand who they are. If they indicate that they will be choosing the agency they believe delivers the best creative work for the pitch assignment, then we likely walk away. Granted, we have all the confidence in the world in our creative abilities. However, this selection criterium indicates that all they care about is the end result, and they have little interest in how to get there. Or it could also indicate that they just don't understand how agencies work and actually fall into the undecided category (this is more likely to be the case if this is the first time this brand has ever selected an agency). If there is a chance this is the case, we will have a conversation with them to determine which bucket they fall in. If we determine that they are undecided, we will proceed only if we are in a position to allocate the appropriate amount of resources without too much pain and we believe the opportunity is worthwhile (i.e., potential for a long-term relationship, good creative opportunity, or financial reward).

The reality is that the new business-pitch process is not a true representation of how an agency works. Similar to most service businesses, the client-agency chemistry is the most important part of any successful relationship (once again, it is about shared beliefs). And when a new business pitch doesn't allow for that to come out, it demonstrates that the client doesn't share that same belief. The agencies that can afford to participate have the greatest advantage, even though they may not be the best fit for the client. Those agencies that don't have the resources available go in at a disadvantage, and the work can often suffer (since they need to focus their energies on paying clients). And often times, the agency that does the best is the most desperate agency—one that recently lost an account and has their inactive staff working around the clock to desperately save their jobs. Yes, the most desperate agency has the advantage.

Perhaps the best gauge to determine if your moral truly connects with your audience is whether you would be willing to hang it on the wall of your lobby or business location. Unlike the positioning or mission statement that many organizations put on badges and break-room posters for their employees to recite, this open display of the moral can serve as a litmus test for everyone who may be a part of the brand story. Those who agree with the moral will feel an immediate sense of belonging. Those who don't disagree may not immediately feel a strong connection but will be open to learning more. And those who don't agree will immediately recognize that they don't belong and are welcome to turn around and go right out the door they came in through—they are not worth the time trying to convince otherwise.

In the lobby of Small Army, you will find the words "The strongest relationships are built upon shared beliefs." For everyone who works there, it serves as a constant gut check and reminder of what we stand for and why we are there. For those with whom we have relationships—clients, partners, and others—it is a reminder of our shared connection. And for those with whom we are considering a relationship, it is an immediate test to see if we belong together. If they do not believe it, we will gladly introduce them to another agency they may be more suited to work with.

CHAPTER 8
RECOGNIZE WHAT REALLY MAKES YOU UNIQUE

"With our product, it only takes two clicks to make this change. With theirs it takes three," I recall a product manager from Dassault Systèmes SolidWorks Corporation telling me when I asked about the difference between their product, and the competitors'.

"But what happens when they change that in their next version?" I asked, knowing features and functionality are most often only a temporary differentiator.

After many conversations like this one, we quickly confirmed that the features and functionality of most three-dimensional computer-aided design software (3D CAD), used by engineers to design and test products before they get built, are similar to one another. Although DS SolidWorks was one of the first to market a desktop 3D CAD system many years earlier, its primary competitors were catching up. DS SolidWorks needed to differentiate itself beyond features and functionality as the market was approaching commoditization.

During our discovery process, we began to learn a bit more about the company. Founded by a brilliant former MIT student (who was also one of the poker players featured in the movie *21*), DS SolidWorks provides software to help engineers design great products (the happily-ever-after). DS SolidWorks recognized that engineers rarely worked alone. Just like the group of poker players in *21*, engineers worked in teams, often across the globe, to share ideas, create interrelated parts, test designs, and manufacture products. DS SolidWorks was helping these engineers work together effectively. An online gallery enabled users to upload and share designs with one another. Small user groups existed in communities all over the world, where users would come together to share ideas and talk shop. And DS SolidWorks hosted a large annual user conference where thousands of loyal users would come together to listen to inspirational talks from other engineers, learn about upcoming feature enhancements, provide feedback and recommendations for future product functionality, and, of course, share ideas and collaborate with other users.

I remember going to their user conference for the first time and watching engineers rip off their button-down shirts at the registration desk to put on the new branded t-shirts they received when they signed in. These people loved this brand—and it was not just because of the technology. As we spoke with the users, we learned that they viewed DS SolidWorks as not just software, but as a true partner who, along with many other engineers, was helping them create great designs. DS SolidWorks, like its customers, believed that people can create amazing things when they work together (the moral of the story). This belief is what ultimately set them apart.

Brands often look far and wide to identify what differentiates them from their competition. They compare features and functionality, pricing, processes and techniques, raw materials, contractual terms, and other details to reveal the differentiators.

Often times, brands will tell us they have already done considerable competitive analysis, and they send over detailed spreadsheets with this information. This information is helpful—especially for product managers who need to make sure their products keep up with the market. However, this information can also change with the wind—it is not what truly makes the brand unique. If it is, it won't be for long. If it's that special, someone else will find a way to replicate it or do it better—even if you do have a patent on your unique approach. The other bank will come out with a better rate. The other ad agency will add a new capability. The other coffee shop will see your free-trade coffee and raise you a fresh-baked croissant. The toilet-paper brand will do four-ply shortly after you launch three-ply. Or the other software company will do your two clicks in only one click. Features and functionality—just like service and price—are not core differentiators. They are simply the table stakes to compete.

Years ago, I worked with Seniorlink, a large provider of care-collaboration solutions that, among other things, helps families on Medicaid take care of their loved ones—most often an elderly parent or adult child with disabilities—in their own homes. With their primary service at the time, Caregiver Homes, a friend or family member could be trained and compensated to take care of the loved one who needed the care. This caregiver would then be required to provide daily reports through a web-based platform and was supported by an assigned social worker and nurse to help with the overall care.

"Family caregivers are a silent army that form the bedrock of our health-care system. They deserve support. Our focus on the caregiver is what makes us unique—no one else really does what we do," the founder, Byron, shared with me.

However, by no means did this imply there was no competition. When families on Medicaid seek assistance for a loved one, they are most often referred to nursing homes and rehab centers.

In-home care is often insufficient, unaffordable, or simply not standard procedure. And in the case of Seniorlink's Caregiver Homes, the service may not even be available.

Since Caregiver Homes was being funded through Medicaid, Seniorlink had to get legislative approval to provide their services on a state-by-state basis. In order to do this, they needed to do more than share how they were different. They needed to communicate why they were different—not only to potential customers, but to legislators (for approval to provide services) and referring professionals (hospital workers, lawyers, Medicaid professionals, and so on) to point prospects in their direction.

In speaking with their customers, we learned that many of them had been caring for a loved one for many years but, due to worsening health conditions, financial hardships, or other conditions, they needed support. They were sickened by the thought of sending their loved one away from home to a place where strangers would provide care, but felt like they had no other choice. Many of them even shared horror stories about the places they were forced to send their loved ones before they discovered Caregiver Homes.

"Caregiver Homes kept my family together," one caregiver shared as tears ran down her cheeks.

After much discovery among customers, legislators, referrers, and employees, we identified the moral of the story: "No one can care for family like family."

With this moral, Seniorlink was able to quickly share what truly made them unique in the market, giving good reason for legislators, referrers, and prospects to consider their unique approach. It was not about *how* they did it, it was about *why* they did it. Once they communicated that, everyone who shared their belief was all ears on learning more.

Seniorlink built on the success of this finding, keeping families and family caregivers at the heart of what they do as they expanded into building technology-driven solutions for care coordination.

The success of their solutions in the face of thick competition, Byron says, owes much to the moral center of the brand remaining strong.

Brands have many different competitors. They compete not only with products and services that are similar, but also every alternative approach that may prevent someone from building a relationship with them. A local coffee shop doesn't compete only with other coffee shops, they also compete with home brewing. Nonprofit organizations compete for support from others with similar missions, along with virtually every other organization that is asking for a share of someone's philanthropic dollars. In the case of Seniorlink, it was nursing homes and rehab centers.

In order to ensure that the moral of your story is unique in a market, you must understand where the alternative options put their stake in the ground. Brands do not generally state the moral of their story. It is implied through their words and actions. Therefore, to identify the moral of the alternative stories, you must experience them. Visit their websites not only to find out what they do, but also read and listen for what they seem to believe is most important. Sign up for their e-mails. Join their social-media communities. What are they placing the most emphasis on? Look at the background of the founders and executives to understand where their beliefs may lie. Read interviews and watch videos of the leadership, where the unscripted moral may reveal itself. Review their philanthropic efforts to understand what really matters to them in their heart. Go to their stores and speak with sales representatives as though you were interested in becoming a customer—and listen for what parts of their products and services they emphasize the most. Open an account. Buy their products. Experience their experiences. And of course, ask why. Eventually, you will see where their hearts may lie.

Sage Bank is a small community bank in the largely blue-collar mill town of Lowell, Massachusetts. Of course, with banks on virtually every corner, this is an industry in which it is seemingly impossible to differentiate. From the large international and national brands to the smaller community brands, they all generally offer the same products—checking and savings accounts, money-market accounts, mortgages, home-equity lines of credit, small-business loans, and so on. The services are becoming ubiquitous—free ATMs, online checking, and mobile banking—and they're all very proud of the philanthropic work they do for their communities.

When we began working with Sage Bank, they had already conducted a fairly comprehensive analysis of their competitors, identifying some gaps and weaknesses in their products and services, and they were already doing what they could to address those gaps. In some cases, they couldn't compete. The larger banks had more money to lend, and their global presences enabled them to provide stronger international services. But in the city of Lowell, few are looking for $50 million loans and doing significant business overseas.

As we studied the market and dug into the alternative solutions, speaking with sales representatives, interviewing customers (asking "Why?"), and reviewing their communications, we found that most of the banks they competed with lacked a clear moral. The customers we spoke with in their communities couldn't really identify anything that made their banks unique. Those doing business with the large banks often applauded the technology but complained about the service, while those with the smaller banks often shared the opposite perspective.

In reviewing competitive advertising, we found that most banks were all sharing similar stories: low interest rates on loans, high interest rates on deposits, and low fees on checking accounts. Their websites and marketing materials went a bit deeper, promoting the great convenience of ATMs, branches, online banking, and mobile deposits. And, of course, they all proudly displayed pictures of themselves in the community, handing out checks to needy nonprofits and giving balloons to kids at their booth at the local fair. Strip the colors and the logos and they were all virtually saying the same thing. Lots of swagger, yet little soul.

However, with each bank we looked at, we interpreted a moral to the story they were sharing. Perhaps the most compelling—and clearly communicated—of them all was Bank of America, which demonstrated that "Life is better when we're connected." Even the nice representative we invited to our offices offered to connect us with some other people in our industry. This was clearly a belief that they not only lived by but tried to demonstrate in all aspects of their business—and it is one that many individuals, especially business professionals, could connect with.

For most of the others we looked at (primarily other community banks), the morals were much more difficult to identify. They were clearly confused brands, but we tried to make sense of their stories. We inferred that one bank believed "an entrepreneurial spirit creates success." While that may have been somewhat compelling, it's not necessarily true. Another bank believed that "community members must support one another." While very kind, it doesn't really lead you to a happily-ever-after. And another caused us to conclude that "more is better," as they just promoted everything they could in every place they could tell you—although they didn't seem to have anything more than any other bank was offering.

In our meetings with Sage Bank, we felt something unique from the moment we walked in the door. They were not dressed in suits and ties (as they were at most other banks). Their products and services were competitive, yet honestly not any more special than the other banks. They were proud of all the work they did in the community, and it authentically felt like something they wanted to do as opposed to something they felt obligated to do. But what struck us most was the way they all spoke about their colleagues and customers.

Branch managers shared stories of visiting the homes of elderly customers who couldn't make it to the bank to help them make a deposit or teach them how to use online banking. Loan officers told us how they helped small businesses in which they saw potential, even when the numbers indicated otherwise. They may not have given them a loan right away, but they took the time to help them with advice and connections so they could further develop their businesses. Then, when the business was ready, Sage Bank would help them with banking services, and they would be right by their side to make sure they succeeded along the way.

Sage Bank truly believes in the people they serve—employees, customers, and the community.

"I was in high school when I started here," Carlos told us with great pride. "But they kept giving me more responsibilities, and now I'm in the marketing department. They really took me under their wing."

They are driven to help everyone prosper. They provide more than the typical banking products and services that are expected. They invest their time and resources into each and every customer they serve and employee they hire. They do this because, like the people they serve, Sage Bank believes "We do well when those we invest in do well." That's a bank I'd want to bank with.

The moral of your brand story must be yours and yours alone. Other brands may believe it, but they do not live by it. While two organizations may share some beliefs, their individual core belief—the moral of their story—is almost always different. It is rare that a brand shares the same core belief with its competitors, as souls are truly unique. Even twins who look the same, dress the same, act the same, and were raised the same way ultimately have their own unique souls. When you look deep inside your brand, you will realize it truly is different from those around you. Ducati probably believes that "freedom is exhilarating," but they do not let that define them as Harley-Davidson does. DS SolidWorks' competitors likely agree that "people can create amazing things when they work together," but it is not the core belief that drives them. Nursing homes and rehab centers may agree that "no one can care for family like family," but their business models surely do not reflect it as Seniorlink does. And like Sage Bank, most every bank would likely agree that "we do well when those we invest in do well." However, Sage Bank took ownership of it. They even re-branded the bank "The Bank of Interdependence."

What truly makes a brand unique is not how they do what they do, but why they do what they do. The moral must reflect this. And once a brand discovers that differentiating belief, they must put their stake in the ground to own it and live by it. In doing so, they will rise above the alternatives and attract people who share that belief with them.

CHAPTER 9
KEEP IT SIMPLE

In the early 1990s, I joined a small marketing agency in Boston that worked solely with high-tech companies. This was years before the Internet. We didn't have iPhones, and ninety-eight percent of the world was using PCs—most with Windows 2.0. Technology was anything but simple. And it was part of my job to understand what each of our clients did—from disk storage and multimedia software (CD-ROMs) to hard-disk optimization and memory.

As I sat in meetings with senior executives and product managers, my head would quickly begin to hurt. Not only was the technology difficult to comprehend, but my colleagues were literally speaking a different language. They tossed acronyms about as though they were as well-known as *IRS* or *FBI*. They referenced industry terms as though they were part of a second-grade vocabulary and used completely made-up words and phrases as though *Webster's Dictionary* were just slow to catch up. I felt like I needed a glossary to follow along (and, on more than one occasion, the company had one that they gave me).

During the first few meetings, my head hurt too much to ask questions. I would leave these meetings wondering what had just happened, hoping one of my colleagues understood at least a fraction more than I did—and hoping he or she could explain it to me later in words I could understand. Only after I had a few aspirin.

Fortunately, many of my colleagues were able to follow along. They were some of the smartest people I had ever worked with, and I was often impressed at how they could not only keep up in these meetings but even ask seemingly intelligent questions. But the deeper they got into the businesses, the more they also began to speak a language that I could not understand, and it began to show in everything our agency did for them.

As years went on, I found it wasn't just the technology companies that had created their own language. Virtually every business develops their own internal language that, over time, becomes commonplace within the organization. The reality is that marketing people are often the creators of it. In an effort to "simplify" the story, or make it interesting, they begin to use words and phrases that are not common to the rest of the world. I mean, how many times do you use words like *synergistic, multifunctional,* or *cannibalize* in your day-to-day conversation? But they sound so big and important.

I used to feel ignorant about this language divide. And like my former colleagues, I would work hard to learn the language so I could speak equally intelligently in these meetings. But over time, I learned that this approach would be detrimental to the brand. While you can teach a new language to employees and partners who are already on board, it is not an effective approach for building relationships with new people.

So, rather than keeping my mouth shut and waiting to learn later, I became an advocate for the common people. With each acronym that was used, I would ask for a definition—which then often required a further definition of the words that made the acronym. With each term I didn't understand, and with each made-up word or phrase, I would ask for the meaning. I would make it into a game and had fun calling people out for speaking in a different tongue. The more I called it out, the more people realized why they had a hard time speaking with customers and prospects.

Marketing professionals are often the greatest cause of this second-language phenomenon. We find ourselves so deep in industry data and market reports that we begin to adopt the language of analysts. When we come across names that seem too simplistic or elementary, we make up more interesting terms to make them seem more important or beneficial. We create acronyms when we are too lazy to continually say the three or four words that they stand for. And in an effort to sound smarter than everyone else, we use big, wonky words that you learn at business school and read in analyst reports. We then apply this language to our communications and assume we look really smart. Everyone follows along because, over time, this language becomes commonplace to us.

The moral of your story must be something that everyone in your brand's story can easily understand. When discovering the moral of the story, I often imagine the CEO standing up at a podium in front of all the brand's board members, employees, customers, partners, and investors, saying, "We are all here today because we believe [moral of the story]." This one statement should cause each and every person in the audience to feel a sense of belonging. If the members of the audience do not believe it, they are in the wrong place. But if they don't understand it, then the moral is rendered meaningless.

So, I ask one simple question: "Will a first grader understand it?" The moral really needs to be as simple as a moral a child would learn from a fairy tale.

As a parent of two young children, I often test morals on my kids prior to sharing them with a client. I tell them the moral and then ask what it means. When the moral is spot on, they look at me with a big smile, repeat it back to me, and start sharing examples of how it applies to them. This is when I know they get it.

In other cases, they give me a quizzical look and say, "Dad, that doesn't make any sense." I'm used to hearing this from them a lot—not just with morals but with life in general. But this is where a child's mind can also be very helpful. I ask them what they don't understand, and they either pick out the words they are having trouble with or explain why they don't understand the moral. I then try to explain it to them in words they do understand, and as I do that, they help to recraft the statement accordingly. It's not that the moral isn't correct—it is just that the words are not correct. If people can't understand them, then they are meaningless.

Not everyone has the benefit of having young children at home to test a moral, but you must force yourself and others to think like a child in order to get there.

I remember sharing with my kids the moral of the story for the local zoo—one client they were very glad I was working with. The zoo was looking to increase attendance and raise its profile, so they came to us to help them discover their soul and tell their story.

As we spoke with the executives, administrators, zookeepers, veterinarians, and others there, we learned that the attraction part of this zoo was really secondary to the true mission of the organization. While people may often not understand the role of a modern zoo, we learned that this zoo (like all other accredited zoos) was truly there to save and protect the animals that they cared for.

While this concept was not necessarily obvious to zoo visitors, the animals were on display—but they were not there for show. Each animal had a story for why it was there. Beau, the giraffe, was brought to the zoo at a young age when they discovered a wasting disease that caused many giraffes in the wild to die within months. The zoo studied the disease and worked tirelessly with Beau to learn how to manage it. Through a series of trial and error, they found a medical treatment that worked—and twelve years later he is still galloping along, despite every other giraffe with this disease living no longer than three years. They loved and cared for Beau as anyone would love a pet. They knew every detail about him—even the fact that Beau only liked to eat assorted fruit-flavored Tums. Some animals were brought to the zoo after being saved from the illegal wildlife trade. Others were injured in the wild and unable to survive on their own, so the zoo provided a home for them. While the conditions at the zoo were different from their natural habitat, there was no question that the zoo truly cared for and respected these animals.

As we worked to find their moral, we first sought to clarify their happily-ever-after. The executives at the zoo shared grand visions of preserving the natural order of the world, viewing their work as critical to the future of humankind. They ultimately wanted to save the world, but this ending did not seem reasonably achievable. A more realistic happily-ever-after for the zoo was to create a world where people enjoy and respect all living beings. This helped ground the zoo and caused them to see themselves in a light their audience could understand. They may not be saving the world, but their work can help everyone enjoy and respect all living beings. And with that respect, people will be more inclined to take care of them and do what's right to save and protect all those who inhabit our planet.

With the happily-ever-after as our beacon, we began throwing moral statements on the wall.

"When we see how others live, we respect their place in the world."

"When you understand the natural order, you respect it."

"Respect happens when you understand the whole story."

We were in the right place, but the words were not right, so we began dissecting the statements to get to the essence of the moral in much simpler terms. It boiled down to four simple words:

"Respect comes from understanding."

When I got home that evening, I shared this moral with my eight-year-old son and asked him what it meant. He first replied with his usual wise-guy remark, "Another moral, Dad?" and then continued on with "Well, like the more I know about the kids in my class—like where they're from or what they like, the more I respect them." At that point, I knew we had the right moral.

This was the underlying "why" behind everything the zoo did. While the animals were entertaining, that is not why they were on display. They were on display so visitors could learn about them and, in doing so, gain respect for them. The birthday parties for the animals, behind-the-scenes tours, school field trips, and other educational classes were all intended to teach visitors about the animals and share their stories. It was intended to be fun, but most important, everything they did was intended to help people understand the animals and their place in the world so that they would gain respect for them and behave accordingly.

As the zoo moral also demonstrates, the moral is not intended to tell you exactly what the brand does. It is a simple belief that applies to the brand but can also be understood and demonstrated beyond that context. My son applied the moral to his classmates. That was his context. In the case of BMC, many of the patients viewed the moral (life's greatest privilege is taking care of those around you) as giving a friend in need a place to sleep. And with Quincy Mutual, many people who worked there thought about their career choices when reflecting on the moral "the future depends on the choices you make today."

The moral must be simple and broad enough for the audience to interpret it in their own context. It should also cause your audience to assume your strengths—without bragging about them. When people understand that the zoo believes "respect begins with understanding," then they are likely to assume they will learn something when they go there—as opposed to it just being a place of entertainment. They may also assume that the zoo respects the animals and wants others to do the same. If the zoo simply told people, "We respect the animals" (as many do), we might not believe them because we generally don't believe what brands tell us—especially those we do not have a relationship with.

The first-grader test also provides another benefit. Aside from questioning the words, young children always need to know "why." Sometimes, I think children would be better at conducting interviews than most adults, because they rarely accept statements at the surface level. "Because I said so" is never an acceptable answer. For this reason, it is often best to avoid words like *should* or *deserve* in a moral, as those words often demand the question "why." Everyone should have the right to vote. Everyone deserves a second chance. While you may believe in these statements, there is often a deeper reason for it. Why do you believe everyone should have the right to vote? Why do you believe everyone deserves a second chance?

Of course, you can ultimately ask "why" to any statement. The moral should reflect a statement that is satisfactory to all those who live by it and doesn't demand the question "why." Someone may ask, "Why does respect come from understanding?" However, that is kind of like asking, "Why is the earth round?" It just is— and doesn't really need further explanation. If certain people need further explanation, they likely either are not your audience (those who don't agree) or may need some education (those who don't disagree). Move on.

The moral of the story does not need to be written on table tents or placed on the back of employee badges to be memorized or used as a script in case of the awkward "what does your company do" moment. The moral connects with everyone who is associated with it, and it lives within them. They innately remember it because it is true to who they are. It uses words that they use in everyday life. And it has meaning to them.

After presenting the moral of the story to executives, we often move on to other discussions—maybe even go out to lunch afterward. However, before we leave, I always ask them, "What's the moral of your story?" This is my final test to make sure it is correct—and simple to remember. When they don't hesitate or run to look at their notes and confidently recite it back without giving it a second thought, I am reassured the moral is right.

CHAPTER 10
LET THE MORAL GUIDE YOU

In 2013, Associated Early Care and Education called upon Small Army to discover the moral of their story and, ultimately, rebrand the organization. Since launching the first child daycare center in all of New England in 1878, they had grown to become a leader in the development of early childhood education across the United States. Now they were about to embark on their largest initiative yet. They had just received a major grant from the Commonwealth of Massachusetts to build a state-of-the-art learning center in Boston's Bromley Heath neighborhood, one of lowest-income residential areas in Boston. This new learning center was much more than just a beautiful building with fully equipped classrooms, multifunction art and music rooms, a beautiful gymnasium, technology-enabled adult learning rooms, comfortable meeting spaces, an outdoor playground, and full catering facilities. It was designed to serve as a laboratory for early childhood education, testing new curriculums and methods of teaching that could improve the field and then be replicated in other centers—not only in their network but across the world.

But the launch of this new facility brought with it several new challenges. Although the land and construction were being funded through grants, the ongoing maintenance of the facility, along with the staffing and other operational requirements, necessitated that they build deeper relationships with families, donors, community members, and political leaders. The financial subsidies provided by the state could not cover the actual cost to care for the children and deliver the services they sought to provide. They needed the support of others now more than ever. It was time for their story to be told—and they needed a moral to guide them.

As we began our discovery process, we met with executives representing the organization—from the executive director and chief operating officer to board members—and the love for the children and the communities they served was immediately apparent. Many of these individuals credited their early education for their own personal success. They shared stories about growing up in inner-city communities where subsidized care not only provided an early education but also gave their parents the opportunity to go to school or get a job to effectively support their families.

The teachers at the centers shared similar stories. Their input and stories provided even deeper insight into the children and families they were currently helping. I can't remember exactly what they said, but the stories here are representative of those conversations.

Sitting in one of the classes, a teacher pointed out an adorable African American girl. She had a huge smile across her face as paint dripped off her hands and onto the blue smock covering her cute little dress. "Only a few weeks ago, she was living out of a car with her mother," the teacher told us. "But here, we take care of her. We give her three meals each day. And her mother was able to find a job and afford a place to live."

Another teacher pointed out a little Latino boy who was intensely focused on the pile of blocks in front of him as he pondered how to add another without causing them all to fall. "His grandmother is taking care of him right now, while his mother is being treated for drug addiction," the teacher shared with us. She paused and then continued with a frown, "They don't know where his father is."

The stories were endless. And with each one, we began to recognize the true impact of these centers. Childhood education was clearly a top priority. But these centers were doing more than helping the children they served. They were helping entire families. Aside from giving them the ability to find jobs and earn a living, they provided a range of adult learning programs to help families and members of the community with everything from financial management and college preparation to nutrition and resumé development.

As someone who grew up in a middle-class neighborhood just north of Boston, I first assumed that many of these parents hoped to move away from these neighborhoods to find a better place to live. But in speaking with many of these parents, I recognized my naïveté.

"This is our community. It is where our family has always lived," one parent told me. "We don't want to leave here. We just want it to be a safe place for our children to grow up and have opportunities."

As we worked to craft the story for the organization, we first had to acknowledge that their happily-ever-after was bigger than just taking care of children. In fact, it was even bigger than taking care of families. In their happily-ever-after, communities flourished. Their communities.

A few weeks later, as I waited in the meeting room full of leaders of the organization sitting on unfolded chairs around the unfolded plastic tables, I got a bit nervous. I was about to tell this group of passionate leaders that their story was slightly different from the one they'd been telling for over one hundred years. But after speaking with so many people, including many of them, I was confident the story was right. We had discovered their moral, and, on this day, I was excited to reveal it to them. After sharing a summary of our research findings, I began:

Today, many communities do not have the opportunities that others have. Poverty, crime, substance abuse, and other difficult family situations contribute to that. Because of this, these communities suffer, and the constant cycle of inopportunity prevents them from thriving.

Children can change that cycle. When children understand right from wrong, are prepared to learn, have good role models, are shielded from crime and abuse, and are generally put in more nurturing environments, they can and will thrive. When they thrive, those around them thrive—and the cycle changes.

Early education is critical, but it takes more than early education to change a community. It takes nurturing.

And that's what you do here. It's more than early education and childcare. Your adult education, community training, and active pursuit of new and innovative ways to support children and families all contribute to your success. And with your new learning lab in Bromley Heath, you are positioned better than ever to make an impact in communities here and across the country.

You do this because, like each and every person you serve, you believe:

When you nurture a child, you nurture a community.

As I spoke those final nine simple words, tears rolled down the cheeks of many people in the room. They immediately recognized that their happily-ever-after was bigger than a child's development. Their work had the potential to impact entire communities. And it all began with the children.

Until this point, they had been on a journey but had not necessarily had a clear destination or compass to direct them. Now they did. Not only did their moral explain the journey going forward, but it also made sense of everything they had done to get there.

From that moment forward, the moral for Associated served as the foundation for the organization's story. It started with a name change. Just like a person's name, the name of an organization is one of the most sacred and personal elements of a brand—especially one that has been with the organization for such a long time. In fact, at the beginning of the moral discovery process, several board members expressed significant concerns with changing the name and strongly advised against it. However, with their involvement in the process and discovery of their moral, they immediately jumped on board with the new brand name, Nurtury. And along with that, there was a new tagline: "Where kids and communities grow." This was the first of many steps to change the narrative for the organization and represent something even bigger than early childhood education.

Once you identify the moral of the story, you are able to frame the brand story more effectively. The moral gives reason for everything the brand does and, therefore, provides context for any message that may follow. With Nurtury, the moral explained why they took care of children. But it also made sense of the community and adult-education classes, educator training, network of family centers, and new learning lab.

The specific set of messages may be different for any given audience, but the moral premise is the same for all of them. With the moral as your guide, you are able to reframe what you do in a context that your audience will connect with.

Consider Boston Medical Center. They are proud to employ some of the best doctors in the world, have some of the most advanced medical technologies, and treat a wide range of medical conditions. These are among the three most important attributes that every potential patient would likely want to know. However, simply stating these important attributes causes them to sound like every other hospital—especially in a region where almost every hospital can say the same thing. But watch what happens when they lead with the moral.

"At Boston Medical Center, we believe that life's greatest privilege is taking care of those around you."

This simple statement is more powerful than any singular selling point, as it causes the audience to assume positive things about them. Most importantly, it shows that they actually care about the people they treat, which is more important than any other attribute, especially in the communities they serve.

Then, when it comes time to communicate individual messages and selling points, Boston Medical Center can frame them within the context of the moral. Because we believe that life's greatest privilege is taking care of those around us:

- We have experienced physicians committed to taking care of the people in our community.
- We employ the most advanced technology so we can provide the best possible care.
- We treat a full range of conditions, because everyone around us is unique.
- We would like you to book a primary-care appointment.

When what the brand does is put in context of the moral, the audience will more likely respond positively (as long as they are not nonbelievers of the moral). The moral also provides context for an entirely different set of messages for donors. At Boston Medical Center, "we believe life's greatest privilege is taking care of those around you." This is why:

- We treat everyone equally, regardless of race, religion, or financial situation.
- We provide social services such as a food pantry, legal services, tax assistance, and immigration assistance for those who need help.
- Our staff volunteers thousands of hours to provide services above and beyond that which is paid by insurance providers and government subsidies.
- We need your support.

When you begin with the moral of the story (why you do what you do), the audience (especially the believers) will make positive assumptions about what you do.

With about fifteen educators and marketing professionals sitting in a large conference room at Boston University School of Education, I remember presenting the moral of their story, "Every learning moment can change a life." The dean of the school immediately began rewriting his commencement speech to incorporate that statement. However, one person in the room raised her hand (as they do in schools), and asked, "Wouldn't we want to say, 'At BU School of Education, we change lives'?"

This is a common instinct. Marketers tend to think that we need to directly tell people about ourselves and what we do in order for them to understand it. In response to the question, I asked everyone in the room to imagine that there were two billboards in Kenmore Square (an area in Boston just down the street from the school, where the Red Sox play in Fenway Park). One billboard read, "At BU School of Education, we change lives." The other read, "Every learning moment can change a life" and included the BU School of Education logo beneath. They immediately understood. The former feels braggadocios and not believable. The latter connects with people and causes them to assume that BU School of Education creates learning moments that change lives.

I am not sure if the story is myth or truth, but I was once told of an advertising executive who was sitting in a room with a bunch of his colleagues and clients, reviewing a creative brief for an upcoming ad campaign. After the executive presented the one message that they believed to be most important for the campaign, the client responded, "But what about the five other key messages we told you were important?" At that moment, the advertising executive reached into his pocket, grabbed a handful of coins, and as he tossed them into the air said, "Catch!" The client didn't catch any of them and then furiously said, "What did you do that for?" The advertising executive smirked and responded, "Because that is what you are asking us to do with the ad. If you throw too much at someone, they won't catch anything."

The reality is that both the client and the advertising executive have good points. Rarely is there one key feature, function, benefit, or attribute that will cause every person to consider purchasing a product. Or, by focusing on the one message that seems to have the greatest appeal, the brand limits its impact, as some of the audience would be more interested in another message. Instead, share the moral of the story. By doing so, the audience will either assume the positive attributes or be open to learning more about them.

The world's most loved brands communicate this way. Of course, there are times when they have a specific message they need to share. However, they recognize that selling products begins with building relationships. So when it comes to marketing, rather than leading with key messages, they lead with what they believe—the moral of the story. This is what connects them with their audience, causes them to feel positive, and builds a relationship with a brand. Once that connection is made, the audience will be more open to additional learning through a conversation with a sales representative, a website, an e-mail follow-up, or other communication. There is definitely a time and a place to get into the details with your audience—but if you force it on them too early, you risk them turning away too quickly.

In 2001, billboards showed silhouettes of people dancing with slick white headphones connecting a small white device to their ears. The iPod represented one of the most significant technology advancements of our time, yet the ads said virtually nothing about the technology. Instead, they screamed "simple is better," without saying a word. The audience assumed that this product would be fun and cool and would enable us to listen to music like we'd never listened before. We wanted to learn more and opened up to more detailed messages because we liked the brand. This is when many people fell in love with Apple.

Every brand is on a journey to happily-ever-after with its audience. The moral guides them by informing what they do and explaining why they do it. Let this framework serve as your storytelling platform for building relationships with people. And begin by being a brand that people want to be associated with. In the next section, using the moral as your guide, you will learn how to let your brand's soul shine through and build relationships with people.

SECTION THREE

Let Your Soul Shine Through

CHAPTER 11

BE HUMAN

For many years, I worked with brands to define their personalities. We would hold long meetings with key executives of the organization where we would ask them to list attributes that describe their brand. We'd ask questions like "If your brand were an animal, what would you be and why?" Or, depending upon the crowd (and to mix it up a bit), we'd ask them to compare the brand to a car.

"We're fast and nimble like a Jaguar."

"We're a Honda Accord—not luxury, but highly reliable."

"We're a Mercedes—we don't compromise on quality."

These conversations would be lots of fun as I watched executives furiously debate whether they were a lion or a bear. However, after years of doing this—and watching each person make a case—I realized it was an exercise in futility. They all had good points, and they were all accurate. But great brands don't behave like cars or animals. Great brands act human.

Just like humans, brands have a range of personality traits. Different traits present themselves in different situations. For example, a comedian may be very funny at times, but that doesn't mean he or she is going to tell jokes at a funeral. Or a surgeon may be very intelligent and knowledgeable in the operating room, but you may not want him or her playing on your team in Trivial Pursuit. There are times to let your hair down and others that call for a much more composed presence. It all depends on the situation.

Simply creating a list of personality traits for a brand can potentially have a negative effect, as it causes brands to act the same way all the time, regardless of the situation. This is not how humans act—nor is it how brands should act. It is boring. It is robotic. It is constraining. And it can be unattractive.

Years ago, I attended South by Southwest (SXSW), a large music, film, and digital-technology conference in Austin, Texas. The digital-technology part of the conference is loaded with speakers and events, teaching hungry professionals about digital marketing, social media, new technologies, analytics, and all else digital—so much so that you break a sweat just from reading the session options. While scanning the massive list of panels, I was drawn to one about *content marketing* and *storytelling*—potentially two of the most overused and misunderstood words in the industry (but it did grab my attention and pushed me to attend). As I entered the room, I saw about two hundred people listening intently and tapping out notes on their iPads as the panelists talked about their storytelling and content-marketing successes.

At one end of the table was a panelist who spoke about a series of videos he and his colleagues had created for a major car company. It was a beautifully produced series about a group of young people who took a car across the country and captured their adventures on video—the people they met, the conversations they had, the places they visited, the food they ate, and so on. These videos were shared on a branded website and distributed through several owned social-media channels like Facebook and Instagram and were receiving significant numbers of views, likes, comments, and shares. On the other end of the table, a senior marketing professional at a Fortune 500 company spoke about his team of more than fifty social media professionals who were actively searching the web for content to share, comment on, and engage with. He shared stories about certain posts that commanded millions of interactions.

The audience was in awe of the social media success of these brands and asked many questions about how to produce the content, where to "curate" content (another one of those overused buzzwords), how long it takes to produce it, and so forth. All these questions were interesting and helpful, and each case study was impressive in its own right. But then someone in the audience raised his hand and asked, "How do all the social-media professionals who are curating, creating, sharing, and engaging with the community know what to share and say?"

My jaw dropped as the panelists began answering this question. The first panelist said something like, "We just know when it feels right." The second inferred, "We have good instincts." The third panelist was a bit more honest. He shared his team's lengthy review and approval process for each post and said how challenging it could be to get a simple tweet out the door. As he spoke candidly about their process, the discussion quickly shifted to the challenges of moving quickly in social media. The panelist from the car company admitted to the crowd that the idea for the traveling adventure took several months to get approval. Then, several senior executives had to review each video and post before it was approved to post. And the other panelists revealed that they had a binder of guidelines they followed for all posts and comments, each with specific words and phrases to use in social posts and responses. So it was not quite based on gut and instinct after all.

Whether a brand is represented by five people or fifty thousand people, those individuals need to understand how they must act. There is a time and place for policies, procedures, and thoughtfully planned interactions with audiences. As the examples presented at SXSW demonstrate, successes can still happen. However, when brands are bound by binders of bureaucracy, they can miss real opportunities to build meaningful relationships at the most opportune moments. Brands—and the people representing them—need flexibility to act accordingly in different situations, just as a human would. They need permission to have fun, but they must also know when to be serious. They need the ability to be spontaneous and witty—but they also know when to be quiet and pensive. And they need the opportunity to react and respond quickly. Without this freedom, the ability to build relationships is impeded.

When a brand is guided by its moral, it doesn't need to comply with a list of predefined personality traits. Instead, brand representatives just need to ask themselves one simple question:

"What would someone who believes in the moral say/do?"

With this simple question, the brand gains the ability to act human and behave appropriately in the situation or moment.

In the 2013 Super Bowl, Oreo demonstrated how such spontaneity can pay off. While many brands depended on perfectly crafted, multimillion-dollar television spots to gain the attention of the largest television audience of the year, Oreo literally shined the brightest for almost no money at all. It was the middle of the third quarter of the game, when a power outage in the Superdome caused the lights to go out for more than a half hour. Quick to respond, Oreo tweeted "Power out? No Problem," along with a graphic of an Oreo cookie with the headline "You can still dunk in the dark." This one tweet was shared more than any other Super Bowl tweet and, perhaps best of all, received at least as much attention from the media as any of the other paid Super Bowl television commercials (which were carefully crafted, reviewed, and produced for ridiculous sums of money).

The moral of the story serves as the true moral compass for the brand and enables all those who represent the brand to be spontaneous. In the case of Oreo, a brand representative simply needs to ask: What would someone who believes "it is liberating to be open" say/do? Oreo has embraced the idea of openness (coming from opening the cookie to reveal the inside) and associated that with a positive, liberating feeling. The notion that you can still dunk an Oreo in the dark aligns perfectly with that belief.

We are attracted to humans because of their personalities, and the same holds true for brands. However, our personalities are not a rigidly defined set of attributes. Our personalities are simply a reflection of our souls—and the moral of the story guides us on how to reveal it.

At Swissbäkers, after we discovered the moral, we immediately began considering how they might present the brand differently based on their belief in the moral "every moment counts." Our eyes immediately focused on the posters hanging in the front windows of the restaurant, promoting the new quiche recently added to the menu. The poster had a beautifully lighted picture of a mouthwatering quiche and the words, "Try our quiche made with fresh eggs, vegetables, and cheese. Only $7.99." Every message they wanted to convey was clearly stated in the poster—the ingredients, the price, and the call to action. *But it lacked personality.*

I asked Thomas and his family how someone who passionately believed that "every moment counts" would potentially present that quiche to someone. Thomas looked up at the ceiling, thought for a brief moment, and, in his deep Swiss accent, with a big smile on his face, said "Savor the moment." Without saying the ingredients or even promoting the price, those three words, accompanied by a picture of the quiche, conveyed a much more compelling story. They shared how Swissbäkers really felt about the quiche. The words would connect with an audience who wanted to enjoy the moment. And even without hearing about the ingredients, the audience would assume the quiche is fresh and tastes great. (Although those features could also be added as less prominent copy points for those interested in reading on.) The moral forced

Thomas to think about the food beyond the ingredients and put it in the context of a belief. And in doing so, the result showed personality.

When brands are passionate about their moral, their personality will shine through and they will feel more human. However, aside from being passionate about their moral, I have found two other human traits are ever present in the brands we love: confidence and humility.

At some level, these traits contradict one another. However, more importantly, they balance one another. All confidence and no humility makes for a very annoying brand (and person). And all humility and no confidence can potentially hide a brand's most important accomplishments. However, brands shine and attract people when they have the right combination of both. I call it humble confidence.

Every year, the Greater Boston Chamber of Commerce names one company as the Top Small and Growing Business in the region. When the fast food restaurant B.GOOD won the award in 2014, they didn't rush to issue a bragging press release. Instead, they took the opportunity to thank their customers for helping them achieve this milestone. By way of e-mail, social media posts, and posters in their stores, they thanked their audience for helping them and, as a way to demonstrate their thanks, added a free meal to each of their rewards accounts. Customers proudly shared the news with their networks—not only because they got a free meal, but because they felt like they also won the award. Although B.GOOD clearly let everyone know that they won the award, they did so by giving their customers credit for the achievement. This is humble confidence.

Humble confidence does not just apply to awards. A few years ago, I was away on a business trip with some colleagues in Houston, Texas. I had never been to the area before, so we decided to jump online to check out some restaurant reviews before choosing a place for dinner. We found a restaurant that grew their own herbs and vegetables on the premises, had some great reviews, and didn't look too stuffy for a few work friends to grab dinner together. When we arrived, we were seated at the end of a long community table where other groups were already enjoying the meal. The table was directly in front of the kitchen area, where from my seat I could watch the chef and staff carefully preparing each meal. I watched them cutting each ingredient, listened to the sizzle as the food hit the pan, and watched the flames shoot into the air as everything cooked. Before a meal was placed on the counter for the waitstaff to take it to the table, each plate was carefully cleaned and dressed with garnish. As I watched, I couldn't help but grow hungrier and more excited for the meal to arrive. But above all, I knew it was going to be a great meal. The kitchen staff didn't say anything, but they had the confidence and security to do all the cooking directly in front of the guests. They had nothing to hide and nothing to be uncomfortable about. They were clearly proud of what they were creating and put it on display for anyone to see. It was more than an eating experience—it was a show. But that is not what truly stood out about this restaurant.

On the front of the menu, they told a story about how the restaurant started and the beliefs that led them to use local organic food. They mentioned some of the local farmers they worked with and why they selected them. With every menu item, they listed where the ingredients came from; it wasn't just about their cooking, it was about the ingredients' origins. But then the ultimate surprise came: on the back of the menu, I found a list of the owner's favorite restaurants in Houston, with an encouragement to visit them. That's right. On the back of the menu, the owner listed his competitors with addresses and a personal recommendation on what he liked to eat there. He clearly didn't view them as competitors. Instead, he recognized that his clientele appreciated great, fresh, organic food. Rather than telling everyone why his restaurant was better than all the others, he encouraged them to try other restaurants. He believed strongly in the benefits of organic food and knew he wasn't the only source of it, so he helped his customers— who he knew shared his belief—satisfy their desire.

Some marketing professionals would say he was out of his mind for doing this. I thought it was brilliant. And human. It showed a level of confidence that few are bold enough to demonstrate, while also humbly admitting there were other great restaurants nearby as well. This owner was actually providing a service to his customers while quietly letting them know how confident he was in his own product. That is humble confidence.

Confident brands don't tell people how great they are. They demonstrate it in their actions. They are confident, humble, and passionate about their beliefs. Their moral shines through. This is what attracts us to them, and this is how great relationships are formed. So, rather than creating a list of personality traits, consider how someone who passionately believes in the moral may act in different situations. And always do it with humble confidence.

CHAPTER 12

BE INCLUSIVE

A few years ago, when I was planning a family trip to Venice, I asked my brother, who had recently been there, for some advice as to where to go. He shared a few restaurant recommendations with me but basically said that most all of them were good. Of course, he recommended that we go to Piazzo San Marco, get a tour of Saint Mark's Basilica, and visit the Doge's Palace. But the one recommendation I did not expect was that of a small bookstore in the middle of the Jewish ghetto in Venice. He told me they had a great assortment of Judaica books and art from all over the world. More importantly, he encouraged me to go there because his business card was hanging on the wall of the store. He even gave me the approximate location to look for his card on the wall. So I had to go.

Upon arriving at this bookstore, which couldn't have been more than six hundred square feet, I realized the walls were covered in business cards from thousands of visitors from all over the world. In this single display, created by customers, the store literally showed everyone who visited that Judaism can be celebrated everywhere.

As I searched for my brother's card, I noticed that others in the shop were doing the same thing—and while doing so, we were each discovering the many unique books and pieces of art from all over the world. As soon as I found my brother's card, I took one of mine out of my wallet and posted it next to his. (I apologize now to the person whose card I covered, but there were no blank places left.) I then took a photo, texted it to my brother, and shared it on Facebook. Immediately, I felt like I was a part of this place— helping to share our story—and I couldn't leave without buying something.

As brands discover the moral of their stories, they recognize that their customers are not only consumers of their story but a part of it. They share your moral and want to join you on the journey to happily-ever-after. When this common bond is acknowledged and celebrated, the audience gains a greater appreciation of the relationship. They view themselves as part of the brand, are proud to be a part of it, and, often, feel obligated to promote it and support it—simply because the brand supported them.

When Robert Lewis Jr. started The BASE, an inner-city baseball program in Boston, I couldn't help but want to help him out. I met Robert when he was leading the StreetSafe program for The Boston Foundation—one of the largest charitable foundations in the Boston area. Robert and StreetSafe were working to keep Boston's streets safe by hiring former gang members to informally patrol neighborhoods and mediate conflicts.

Shortly after meeting Robert, he invited me on a late-night tour of Boston's inner city, where he and several members of his street team could introduce me and a few others to the real streets of Boston. As I arrived for the tour, Robert's face lit up, and he gave me a huge hug hello.

"Tonight you'll see what Boston is really all about," he told me.

As I waited for the tour to begin, I chatted with a few other people in the room—an eclectic mix of about fifteen white, black, and Latino adults all with different reasons for being there and different understandings of what was about to follow.

As we prepared to go on our tour, Robert stood up at the front of the room. He started by acknowledging each person in front of him. First, he introduced us to the few StreetSafe team members who would be joining us on the tour. Then, he called out each of the people he invited on the tour and shared why he was honored to have us join him. I immediately felt like I was part of something incredible. Then, recognizing the somewhat cautious faces in front of him, he began with a few words of comfort.

"You have nothing to fear tonight. The people you meet will view you as a jury."

It was an interesting perspective, and definitely one I had never considered. We looked like a jury. And for many of the people we were about to encounter, a courtroom was one of the only places where they would ever see such a diverse group of people together.

Robert continued, "Just show them respect, and they will show you respect right back."

We then got in the van, staring at one another with anticipation. We drove from housing project to housing project, meeting gang members in their neighborhoods. As we got off the van, Robert approached these young men and hugged them, just as he had done with me. He then introduced each of us to these men, and they showed us the same respect they showed Robert. I immediately gained credibility because they knew I was with Robert. I never could have imagined this Jewish, middle-age white guy feeling comfortable in the middle of a gang neighborhood—but somehow I did.

During the tour, I was speaking in the van with one of the StreetSafe team members about his previous gang experience when he was interrupted by a phone call. He told me he had to run but would hopefully meet back up with us later. I didn't ask questions and just continued on. Later that night, when we all met back up at the community center to talk about our experience, my new friend came back. When I asked him if everything was OK, I was taken aback by his response.

"Yeah, it's fine," he told me. "Someone in a gang shot at another guy in a rival gang. Fortunately, they missed. But I needed to get over there to find out what happened and make sure the rival gang didn't retaliate. Better that I go over there than the cops. They trust me. I think it'll be OK."

The moral of the story for StreetSafe became very apparent that evening: "When you give respect, you get respect." Not only did I witness it among the gang members, I experienced it myself. That evening, I became a part of the story—and immediately felt a deeper connection to it.

When Robert left The Boston Foundation, I was compelled to follow him to his next venture. In the late 1970s, Robert had started the Boston Astros baseball program to keep young people out of trouble by introducing them to baseball, giving them discipline, and showing these young men what they could accomplish when they put their minds to it. Robert had led the team to several national championships, and, after years in the corporate world with The Boston Foundation, he decided to take the baseball program to the next level by creating a nonprofit organization called The BASE. He was now able to dedicate himself full time to these young men, growing the organization to serve more than eight thousand men and women across six hundred teams. But it was much more than a baseball program. Robert worked with local schools, colleges, and universities to get education, tutoring, and scholarships for these men. He raised millions of dollars from organizations like New Balance, Franklin Sports, and State Street to get equipment, uniforms, and facilities where they could practice. And not only did he keep these young men off the streets, he created much-needed role models for other young men to follow.

Robert was more than a mentor to the kids on the team. He was their inspiration. They looked up to him like a father. He believed in them like no one else. And for many of these young men and women, they needed desperately for someone to believe in them. So when it came time to discover the moral of the story for The BASE, we agreed that it wasn't about baseball. While a few of the young men went on to pursue major-league baseball careers, professional baseball wasn't the endgame. The endgame was achieving what they wanted to achieve in life. The BASE gave them the confidence, discipline, and opportunity to get there because, as Robert showed them each and every day, "When you believe you can, you can." That's the moral of the story.

Today, this moral serves as the driving force behind the program. Staff, donors, volunteers, and participants are constantly reminded to believe they can—and, of equal importance, to believe in those in the program. They all thrive on one another. When you are surrounded by people who openly believe in you, you believe in yourself. And when you believe you can, you can. Of course, with countless national championship trophies, college degrees, and successful men and women to show for their efforts, they continue to demonstrate this every day.

Today, The BASE doesn't call their supporters "supporters." They don't call their coaches "coaches." And they don't call their players "players." Everyone who is part of their story is considered a "Believer." When you go to The BASE, pictures of Believers hang on the wall. Newsletters from Robert feature other Believers and acknowledge their support and contribution to the organization. Their website and social-media pages include endless pictures of Believers, acknowledging them for their support.

Like The BASE, many great brands recognize their audiences as though they are part of a special club. This recognition causes them to feel a closer bond with the brand. They are part of a community who share a belief or passion that connects them. In Boston,

Red Sox fans are part of Red Sox Nation. Green Bay Packers fans are considered Cheeseheads. Jimmy Buffet fans are Parrotheads. TJ Maxx has Maxxinistas. By simply recognizing your audience as part of a special group of people, they feel like they truly belong.

In the case of The BASE, the audience is an extension of the brand itself. In other cases, the audience can actually become the differentiator for the brand. However, you must first discover the moral of the story to determine if that is the case. Many brands specialize in products for a specific niche audience. However, more often than not, that niche alone is not a differentiator, because they often compete with brands who are focused on a similar niche. For example, there are several advertising agencies that focus on a specific industry such as health care. However, they often compete with other agencies that also specialize in health care. Therefore, it is not a differentiator.

The moral of the story often defines your audience in a way that is truly unique from how others view them—or at the very least, different from how other brands have communicated with them. And that often presents an opportunity to lay claim to that audience and stand up as the brand most suitable for a relationship with them. Life is Good, for example, views their audience as optimists, people who believe life is good.

Blue Hills Bank is a regional bank in Massachusetts, competing with an almost infinite number of bank brands—most of which generally provide the same products and services. However, in working with them to discover the moral of their story, we discovered that their core belief had more to do with how they viewed their customers as opposed to how they viewed their products.

As we met with senior executives, lenders, branch managers, and others, they shared a very honest and insightful perspective about their customers. Time and time again, they told us, "People have many other things they'd prefer to do with their time than spend it with a bank."

"New homeowners are much more excited about moving into their new home than they are about getting their mortgage taken care of," the home lenders told us. "We are just one of the many things they need to take care of before getting to what they are really excited about—their new home."

Business lenders shared a similar perspective: "Business owners are looking to expand their business and want to move as quickly as they can to do so. We need to do what we can to help them and make it easy."

Even the branch managers told us that fewer people are visiting the branch for neighborly conversation. They appreciate that the tellers and bank representatives know who they are, but they mostly just want to take care of business and get back to what they do—do their job, take care of the kids, get back to school, and so on.

As we spoke with customers and prospects about banks, we learned that Blue Hills Bank couldn't have been more correct. Generally speaking, people don't look forward to going to the bank. They may appreciate their banking relationship, but they appreciate it most when the bank makes it easy for them to take care of their banking needs—because they have many other important things to do aside from banking. And furthermore, the opposite is true. The most common reason why people switch banks is not because they see a more compelling rate or offer—it is because they had a frustrating experience at their original bank and decided to look elsewhere.

When we landed on the moral of the story for Blue Hills Bank, we realized that perhaps the most compelling aspect of the moral was that it wasn't just defining the bank, but it defined the customers. The belief "good things happen when it all comes together" was the reason Blue Hills Bank did everything they could to help their customers bring everything together. Aside from providing competitive rates and low fees (the table stakes required to compete), Blue Hills Bank empowered their employees to make decisions quickly so that customers didn't have to wade through bureaucracy. They provided mobile and online banking tools so customers could quickly and easily take care of their banking at any time. And they were able to connect customers with other resources such as real estate brokers, accountants, and lawyers who could support their greater needs.

And more important, the belief defined the customers. They had a lot to do to achieve their goals—whether it be expanding their business, buying a new home, going to college, taking a vacation, or preparing for retirement. Banking was just one of those things that needed to come together for good things to happen. By viewing the audience through the lens of the moral—as opposed to a demographic—we were able to define them in a way that acknowledged all that they had to do and celebrated their accomplishments. We called them Go-Getters and built the brand around them.

It started with a tagline that recognized the needs of the audience: "Work Hard. Bank Easy." Then, rather than having the bank tell the story, people learned who Blue Hills Bank was by learning more about the audience they served. We visited Blue Hills Bank customers and profiled them in advertising, social media, and in-branch communications.

Marta, the CFO of a social services agency, was featured in print ads, social media, and other channels with the headline, "Big-Picture-Always-Moving-Make-It-Happen Marta." In a corresponding interview, she shared her passions (time with her kids, fabulous meals, theatre and films), her words to live by ("Mentor your people. Their success is your success."), how she defined a go-getter (someone who starts with the big picture and always does what it takes to get the job done), and why she chose to work with Blue Hills Bank (wanting a bank that gives back to nonprofit organizations like hers). In another ad, we featured

"Do-More-Never-Rest-Keep-Pushing Patrick," the president of a logistics company. He was passionate about Boston College football and running and had a hidden talent of being able to milk a cow. He defined a go-getter as someone who gets up early, outsmarts the competition, and never gives up. And he chose Blue Hills Bank because he trusted his banker, Patrick, and appreciated the bank's flexibility in working with him.

In radio ads, we shared exhausting stories of go-getters who never stopped going from the moment they woke up to the moment they went to bed—like the mom who woke at the crack of dawn to get her kids ready for school, head off to work, rush home to take the kids to baseball practice, make dinner, read bedtime stories, clean up, and then go to bed.

The customers who were being featured were ecstatic. They felt appreciated by the brand, and their loyalty to it grew stronger. Others were calling and asking how they could be featured. And new customers were referencing the campaign as a reason for choosing the bank—they felt like the bank understood them and would treat them accordingly.

The audience is a critical part of a brand story. When brands acknowledge and embrace this, they demonstrate that they are proud of the relationship. As a result, the audience feels a stronger bond with the brand, and relationships flourish.

CHAPTER 13

BE EMPOWERING

In the 1980s, there was a commercial for Fabergé shampoo featuring the beautiful Heather Locklear as the spokesmodel. With Heather smiling brightly and holding a bottle of the shampoo in her hands, she told the viewers, "I was so excited about the new Fabergé shampoo that I told two friends. And then they told two friends, and they told two friends, and so on and so on." As she spoke, the screen filled with a few dozen people who had heard about the shampoo just because Heather started the chain. This was before social media.

Today, through the power of Facebook, Twitter, Instagram, Pinterest, and a range of other social media platforms, almost everyone has the power to tell hundreds of friends about a brand with the touch of a screen. And if one friend tells two hundred friends and they tell two hundred friends and so on, the numbers get very large very quickly. Social media platforms are just the tip of the iceberg when it comes to the power of sharing. Reviews on sites like Yelp and TripAdvisor, comments on media sites like Huffington Post and New York Times, videos shared on YouTube, and virtually any other web content has the potential of reaching millions of people.

In a world where word of mouth is the most credible source of information about any brand, your audience has the potential to be your best friend or your worst enemy.

In 2009, guitarist/songwriter Dave Carroll had been aboard a United Airlines flight when he looked out the window and saw the luggage crew tossing his band's equipment into the cargo area of the plane. When he arrived at his destination, he found his guitar broken. United did nothing to help him, so he wrote a song about it, made a video, and shared it on YouTube. The song, aptly named "United Broke My Guitar," has now been viewed more than fifteen million times.

That wasn't good for United. However, this same power can be used to help brands. Rather than fear the voice of the audience, brands must listen to it, embrace it, and give everyone the power to use it.

The first year we launched Be Bold, Be Bald! we received hundreds of e-mails from participants, cancer fighters, cancer survivors, and family members thanking us for our work and for giving them a way to fight back. It was gratifying to read these messages and know we were making a difference. However, we also received some e-mails and comments on social media that were slightly less appreciative. One individual currently battling cancer shared via e-mail, "This is so insensitive. Losing your hair is not something to make fun of." A sibling of a cancer patient shared, "This is so offensive. I shared this with my brother, and he said that he would never want me to wear that bald cap for him." And in social-media posts where people were posing with bald caps, we received a few comments with the general sentiment, "If you really want to be bold, then shave your head. Wearing a bald cap is a joke."

Although the thousands of positive e-mails were encouraging, the few negative ones definitely put a damper on the excitement. Our first instinct was to ignore them, but that didn't feel like the humbly confident thing to do. We were proud of what we were doing, and, while we accepted people's perspectives, it wasn't going to prevent us from moving forward. So, rather than ignore any negativity, we let people know we were listening. Although there were not tons of negative e-mails, I personally replied to each one, letting the senders know that we heard and understood their perspective. I also shared my own story, reminded them that we were in the fight together, and invited them to continue the discussion with me over the phone if they'd like. Lastly, recognizing that they likely agreed with our moral (true strength pushes vanity aside) but not necessarily the way we were sharing it, we complimented them for being so strong in their fight against cancer. On some level, I expected great debates to ensue. However, almost every person responded with a thank you. Most added an apology for their reaction. And a few even ordered bald caps.

These e-mails also forced us to consider how we could alleviate some of the negative feedback. The entire idea of the event was to let people go bald without shaving their head—something Mike specifically didn't want us to do for him. We recognized that this was less bold than taking out a razor. But wearing a bald cap in public is still a courageous act of solidarity—and we suspected that more people would be willing to wear a bald cap for a day than shave their head.

So rather than change what we were doing, we gave more meaning to the cap itself. In monitoring social-media posts from participants, we noticed that several people were writing on their bald caps and using it as a canvas to share their story, such as:

"For my best friend."
"For my mom."
"Nothing will stop us."

This inspired us and caused us to recognize an insight we had not seen before. Our audience believed that true strength pushes vanity aside—but they also wanted to share their stories with others. And their stories were part of our story.

So, the following year, we decided to help them share their stories. Every bald kit we sent to participants included more than just a cap. It included a marker and a note that encouraged them to write on their caps and share their designs with us. We updated all the marketing materials to include pictures of participants wearing decorated bald caps that shared their stories. And in social media, e-mails, and other communications, we encouraged participants to decorate their caps and share them with us.

The bald cap became more than a replacement for a razor. It became a canvas for participants to share their stories and demonstrate why they believed true strength pushes vanity aside. And it became a piece of art that participants were excited to share. Participants immediately became ambassadors for the event by posting their decorated bald caps on social-media channels, and, in turn, their friends ordered bald caps and did the same.

Even a brand's biggest detractors can help positively influence the brand story and help it get shared, especially once they recognize the shared belief—the moral. But you have to listen to them, engage with them, and empower them to share your story.

There are endless ways to engage your audience and empower them to share your story. Brands often ask people to do things like share their posts, create/upload videos, take/share photos, craft/post articles, and write reviews in exchange for something of value—or, more often, the chance to win something of value. The 2015 Super Bowl had a few good examples of this.

As major car companies like Mercedes, Lexus, and Nissan were spending millions of dollars on television spots in the Super Bowl, Volvo was seeking to relaunch their brand in the US market with their new XC60 Crossover vehicle. However, Volvo didn't have the budgets of the other car companies to compete in television. So rather than sit on the sidelines, Volvo took to social media and leveraged their audience to share their story.

During major live televised events like the Super Bowl, social media activity increases considerably as people actively comment and discuss the event in real time. In the marketing world, it's called second screen viewing. Volvo saw an opportunity to not only get traction on the second screen but potentially shift people away from the first screen. Each time an ad for a competitive car advertiser came on the TV, Volvo invited everyone on Twitter to win a Volvo XC60. All they needed to do was tweet the name of someone who they believed deserved a Volvo, along with a short reason why and the hashtag #volvocontest.

While Volvo didn't necessarily get the reach of a multimillion-dollar Super Bowl television spot, they succeeded in pulling viewers away from their competitors' ads to share the Volvo story. Volvo was the most tweeted car brand during the Super Bowl that year. The interception was also picked up by hundreds of local and national media channels, giving Volvo even greater recognition.

The idea of inviting people to win a Volvo for someone they love (as opposed to for themselves) was spot on to the moral of the Volvo brand story. Although in recent years Volvo seems to have shifted away from their core message of "safety," this campaign helped to remind people that Volvo, like the people they serve, believes that "the lives of our loved ones are the most precious things we have." I'd argue that the hashtag #volvocontest should have been less promotional and more in line with the essence of the campaign (something like #volvolove or #volvo4life), but overall this idea was a brilliant way to activate an audience and get them to share the brand story.

While Volvo was taking viewers away from television ads during the 2015 Super Bowl, McDonald's took quite the opposite approach. McDonald's was one of the most highly mentioned brands in social media during the big game because they gave the audience something to talk about. However, people were not tweeting about Big Macs and french fries. Instead, they were helping spread the McDonald's core belief (the moral of their story) that "happiness makes life better." While McDonald's is clearly in the food (and real estate) business, the moral of their story is not about food. Food is simply one of the means to the end. We can all debate the nutritional value of many items on the McDonald's menu. And we can talk about the sensation of grease coming out of our pores after eating a Big Mac and large fries. But it does taste good. It is fairly inexpensive. Kids get a toy in their Happy Meals and get to play in the playground. And parents don't worry about their kids being a bit too loud or messy. That is happiness—well, at least one version of it.

So, when the Super Bowl kicked off, McDonald's began to spread happiness by tweeting positive messages about the brands that were advertising during the Super Bowl and encouraging others to retweet their posts. Those who retweeted were then entered into a contest to win a prize related to the advertiser. If you retweeted the post about the Jublia ad (a drug for toe fungus), you were entered for a chance to win new sandals and a pedicure. ("Common side effects of the Jublia ad include lovin' clean toenails. RT and you could win designer sandals and a pedi.") Or if you retweeted about the Dodge ad, you had the chance to win a Dodge Challenger.

While it cost McDonald's a significant amount of money in prizes, it was only a fraction of the cost of a Super Bowl ad. And rather than McDonald's spreading the story of happiness, the social media community did it for them for free.

While McDonald's and Volvo leveraged product giveaways to encourage people to share their posts, such incentives are not a requirement. When you have a relationship with someone, sometimes all it takes is a simple ask. However, the content you ask them to share must be something that they find worth sharing.

Social media isn't the only way for people to share your story. Decades ago, there was a department store in Boston called Filene's

Basement—also known by the locals simply as the Basement. As you walked down the stairs to the Basement from Boston's Downtown Crossing area, you were immediately filled with sensory overload from piles of clothing in bins and racks labeled "Women's undergarments," "Men's dress shirts," "Wedding dresses," "Children's pajamas." You name it, and there was a bin or rack for it. And if you could find something you liked—and that fit—you'd be ecstatic, because everything was a great deal. Most items were fifty to seventy percent cheaper than you would find in regular department stores—partly because they were overstock items and seconds, but also because Filene's clearly did not spend much on cleaning and inventory management. During their annual wedding-dress sale, you'd hear rumors of women literally wrestling in the aisles for the gowns of their choice. It was more than a great deal, it was a fun adventure. And when you walked out of there with something, you were proud. Just like Filene's Basement, their audience believed that "it feels great to get a deal."

If that store existed today, you would likely see signs at the checkout registers that encouraged shoppers to take photos of their prize bargains and share them on Instagram, Facebook, Twitter, or their preferred social bragging tool. A post about a great deal from Filene's Basement would likely invite as many comments (and jealousy) from their friends as a photo from a Caribbean beach vacation.

But this was before social media. People didn't have smartphones in their pockets, hundreds of friends on Facebook, or even the ability to brag on Twitter. However, when people completed their transactions, the merchandise wasn't thrown in a cheap paper bag or even a plastic bag with a logo on it. Instead, all Filene's Basement purchases were placed in a nice white reusable plastic bag with handles that, on both sides, read "I just got a bargain!" in big black letters. And of course, it had the Filene's Basement logo. Shoppers proudly walked up out of the Basement and through the streets of Boston with their large bags, letting every other passerby know that they just got a great deal. And then, when they got home and unpacked their merchandise, they saved and proudly reused their "I just got a bargain" bag for anything else they could. For the price of a bag, Filene's Basement turned shoppers into walking advertisements. They engaged their audience and helped them tell their story. It was potentially the best social-media campaign before the advent of social media.

Every customer experience is an opportunity for a brand story to be told to hundreds of people by someone they know and trust. Generally speaking, people do not share boring or unmemorable experiences. For anyone who ever visited Filene's Basement, you know that every experience was a memorable one. But today, unless you want your story to look or sound like United's, it must also be a positive one. Guided by the moral, brands must consider how their story can turn an experience into a share-worthy moment.

When my family first got our dog, my wife was not thrilled. As a cat lover, she was not completely on board with the decision to get a dog, but my kids and I somehow convinced her to get Jasmine, a Golden Retriever puppy. Within a few weeks of Jasmine's welcome, our house was getting destroyed. The baseboards in the kitchen were chewed to dust. The carpet on the stairway was torn apart and ripped off the ground. The backyard was decorated with deep pits beside piles of dirt. The sprinkler system was leaking water through dozens of dog bites. And worst of all, my wife's Maui Jim sunglasses were destroyed.

With the help of a handyman and landscaper, I was able to address most of the destruction, but I could do little about the Maui Jims—so my wife called them and asked if there was anything they could do. The woman in customer service seemed very understanding and asked my wife to send them the glasses so someone could inspect them and see what they could do. One week later my wife received a package that not only contained a new pair of glasses but also a dog bone and a note that read, "Aloha! We thought Fido might like a bone instead of your Maui Jims! Good luck!"

As they say on Maui Jim's website, they believe that "color and light are the key to human experience." They not only fixed my wife's color and light issue, but they showed that they truly cared about the human experience. While my wife was thrilled to receive a new pair of Maui Jims, it was the card that caused her to share the entire experience with her friends on Facebook. And almost every time someone comments on her Maui Jim sunglasses, she repeats the story.

When you empower your audience to share your story, your story will become that much more powerful.

CHAPTER 14

BE GIVING

Over the last few years, I've been sending a blog article via e-mail to all my contacts about every three weeks. Within each article, I share some kind of insight, knowledge, or advice that I believe would be useful to my connections. Typically, the articles are related to marketing, relationship building, leadership, or culture. I don't put any fancy design on these e-mails, and, apart from asking readers to share their comments with me on my blog or via e-mail, I rarely ask for anything.

After sending these out for about one year, I received an e-mail from a sales representative at an inbound marketing company with some advice on my approach. He suggested that I add a graphic header to the e-mail to make sure my message looked good. And he was insistent that I include an offer of some kind in the e-mail. "You need to give people a reason to respond," he wrote. "Otherwise, you are wasting an opportunity."

I agree that in order to get people to respond, a strong offer is important. However, not every interaction should demand a response. Every time I send out an e-mail, I receive numerous responses thanking me for the content and sharing their insights on the topic. I also receive e-mails from people I have not seen or heard from in a while, asking me to get together regarding a potential project, introducing me to someone, or just reconnecting. The most common response I receive are those telling me how they enjoy reading the posts because I am not selling them anything. I intentionally do not include graphic headers because that's what people do when they sell you something. My e-mails look like an e-mail from a friend, because that is what I consider myself in the relationship.

No one enjoys being sold to. However, brand professionals seem to believe that every interaction is an opportunity to sell. The reality is that every interaction is an opportunity to build or break a relationship. And if every time you interact with someone you ask for something, the person will eventually stop listening to you. This is no different in person-to-person relationships. We all have that friend or family member who is constantly asking for help. He needs a ride to the airport. She needs money. He needs help moving. She needs you to watch her kids. After a while, you begin avoiding this person's calls and texts as much as possible.

Relationships with brands are not very different—except for the fact that it is easier to shut out a brand than it is to shut out a friend or family member. When a brand is constantly selling to us, we stop reading their e-mails and avoid their calls—and when they do happen to get our attention, we believe little of what they have to say because we know they are just trying to sell us something. However, when they are generous and viewed as a brand that gives, we are much more open to listening to them and much more trusting of what they have to say.

In order for brands to build relationships with people, they need to contribute to the relationship—not just in the courting stage, but throughout the entire relationship. Of course, many brand professionals will respond to this by saying, "I am contributing to the relationship with my product or service. And customers contribute to the relationship by paying for it." However, that's a transaction, not a relationship. Giving away a free limited-time trial is not giving either. That's a hook, not a worm.

Let the moral guide your giving.

The moral of the Small Army story is that the strongest relationships are built upon shared beliefs, with a happily-ever-after where brands have relationships with people. Therefore, every one of my articles shares experience, advice, and knowledge that is intended to help people build relationships with their employees, customers, friends, and family.

In 2003, MIT launched their OpenCourseWare program. Many higher-education institutions believed it was a crazy thing to do. The organization was literally giving away course information from actual MIT classes and professors—videos, presentations, curriculums, and exams directly from the classroom—for anyone to access. It was all completely free, without any type of registration, and people were encouraged to share the content with others.

By 2014, the website had more than one billion views, 175 million visitors, and about one thousand courses available for free online. Educators, students, and self-learners from around the world were accessing the content to sharpen their skills, prepare for higher-education learning, excel in their fields, or just learn about a subject they would otherwise not have access to.

When we initially met with MIT OpenCourseWare, we asked the leaders of the organization why they were doing this. The most common response was that it was just the right thing to do. They were proud of the fact that people who could not study at MIT were able to learn from MIT. However, as we dug deeper, we learned that there was more to it. MIT is recognized as one of the top technology and engineering schools in the world. However, the institution's ultimate mission is much more altruistic than to be the best school in the world.

The mission of MIT is to "advance knowledge and educate students in science, technology, and other areas of scholarship that will best serve the nation and the world in the twenty-first century." MIT seeks a happily-ever-after for a better nation and world in the twenty-first century. And getting there is not going to happen only through the education of students but also through the general advancement of knowledge. MIT—and in particular, the OpenCourseWare group—ultimately believes (the moral of the story) that "the more we all understand, the more we all discover."

By providing this content, MIT has not only elevated their position as an educational leader, but also has extended and strengthened their relationships throughout the world. The MIT brand has gained much greater global awareness without spending considerable dollars on advertising (free content gets shared). Professors at MIT, previously known within smaller academic circles, have become in-demand celebrities within their fields of study, attracting students to the campus and driving speaking opportunities and providing credibility for grant funding. Alumni are proud to be associated with an organization that is making an even greater impact in the world and are donating to the school and the OpenCourseWare program. And MIT continues to thrive.

For many brand-marketing professionals, the free content is not the surprising part of the MIT model. The fact that they are giving it away without even asking for an e-mail address is what often causes most surprise. When it comes to content, brands tend to demand tit for tat. They think, "We've worked really hard on putting this content together, so if you want it, you need to give us your e-mail information so a sales rep can call you or we can begin bombarding you with e-mails."

The moment we give a brand our information, we expect the sales pitches to start. Therefore, asking people for their contact information in order to get "free" content is a detractor to a relationship. When you don't force it, people feel safer and more trusting.

I recall, years ago, working with an e-tailer that forced users to enter their e-mail address in order to browse the site. The company was so driven to get e-mails that they forced people to give it to them before they could even see what was offered. That is not a good way to start a relationship. When the e-tailer removed the requirement, they didn't get as many e-mail addresses—but sales increased. Imagine if, when Google launched, they required visitors to enter their e-mail address before they could search the web. Today we would all be using Lycos. Give people the option to share their information with you, but don't require it. And make it easy for them to get in touch with you when they may need you.

The idea of giving extends far beyond informative, educational, and thought-leadership content. Give a dose of inspiration. Give a smile.

When it came time to tell the story for DS SolidWorks, we knew that just creating ads around features and functionality would be useless—and potentially only serve to further move the industry toward commoditization. So instead, we created a web-based sit-com about engineers working together—demonstrating that "people can create amazing things when they work together," while also entertaining the audience we wanted to build relationships with. The series, called *3Dudes Gone 3D*, featured a three-person engineering team that was forced to work in a temporary office trailer due to the growth of the company. Each character was based on stereotypical engineers—the young engineer excited to do anything, the experienced know-it-all engineer, and the stern manager trying to keep everything on time and under budget. Each episode was about five to seven minutes long and was kind of a mix between *The Office* and *Big Bang Theory*. Of course, they used DS SolidWorks software at the office, which provided perfect product placement and opportunities to share some features. But that was secondary to the overall plot.

Rather than creating ads that promoted product features, we created ads that promoted the show. The engineering community flocked to it. They watched each episode multiple times, shared them with their friends, and commented on them. We created *3Dudes Gone 3D* posters that people could download and hang in their offices, ringtones they could put on their phones (leveraging some of the funny lines from the show), and even social-media accounts for the characters to interact with the audience. Rather than ignoring ads about features and functionality, the audience was spending time with DS SolidWorks and engaging with the brand.

After the first few episodes had run, the client excitedly called us to report that she was being inundated by calls, e-mails, and on-line posts asking when the next episode was going to be released. When your audience is begging for more, you know you're doing it right.

DS SolidWorks sales were up that year, as they are every year. And the community is still talking about the series.

Until proven otherwise, people expect to be sold to. However, when you demonstrate that you are more likely to give them something they will appreciate than ask them for something, their expectation shifts. They will be more open to hearing from you. In fact, they may even look forward to it and, if they like it, share it with their friends.

CHAPTER 15
EVERYONE IS A STORYTELLER

As I listened to Judd and Craig Rottenberg, the owners of Long's Jewelers in Boston, share countless stories of customers coming into the store with their children, grandchildren, and even great-grandchildren, I could sense the strong sense of pride they had in their family business. They were proud to be considered part of a family tradition for their customers as opposed to just a good jeweler. However, as they noted, it took more than 130 years to earn that status, and with the reigns now in their hands to keep the family business thriving, they needed to be sure to keep that tradition alive.

As we spoke, the conversation often led back to the anxiety and stress often associated with jewelry purchases. They told me how men (and in some cases women) looking for engagement rings would often walk into the store like deer in headlights, sweating from head to toe and looking ready to turn around and run away the moment someone made eye contact with them. These potential customers were considering making not only the most important decision of their lives, but likely also the most expensive one. Others seeking the perfect gift for a loved one would ask hundreds of questions or make multiple visits prior to a purchase in fear of choosing something the recipient wouldn't like. Still others, either purchasing a gift for themselves or adding to their family jewels, stressed about the future of the piece and whether it would last and be appreciated by generations after them.

Long's Jewelers recognized that they were selling much more than jewelry. In many ways, they were selling peace of mind. To do that, they worked hard to educate their customers about jewelry to help them understand exactly what they were getting. They never put pressure on their customers to buy, and they even encouraged them to look elsewhere if they were not comfortable or did not feel they had found exactly what they were looking for. Why did Long's Jewelers do this? Because they believed and understood that "the greatest feeling is getting it right."

Based on this moral, we developed an engagement-ring campaign that shared this sentiment. Billboards on the highway featured a photo of a beautiful diamond ring that simply read, "It's OK to ask for directions." Digital banners recommended, "Before you ask her, ask us." As a way to give the audience something beyond a sales pitch, we created a microsite with creative ideas for proposing—from spelling out "marry me" while playing scrabble to getting down on one knee in the Boston Public Garden. We even created some fun illustrated how-to-guides like "how to ask her father's permission" or "how to hide the ring." All this content was also shared on social media, and some of it was printed and made available to customers in store locations.

But perhaps more important than driving an ad campaign, the moral served as the foundation for employee training. By incorporating the moral into employee onboarding and sales training, team members are constantly reminded why they do what they do and are encouraged to incorporate that into their role. Sales professionals are trained to listen and get to know their customers so they understand their personalities and style preferences—and those of the recipients of the jewelry (who are often different than the buyer). They keep track of these preferences, along with previous purchases, to help their customers intelligently add to their jewelry collection over time. Everyone there values privacy and confidentiality. (We heard stories of sales or customer-service representatives from other jewelry stores leaving messages on home answering machines—not a good idea when a man is living with the woman he is planning to propose to or a husband is planning something special for a birthday.) And they have a favorable return policy to make sure customers always get it right. With Long's, the moral guides much more than a marketing campaign; it guides every employee to appropriately and consistently share and represent the brand story.

The brands that create the strongest relationships with people are those whose moral is consistently shared by all those who represent it. However, brand representatives can become true brand storytellers only when they understand the moral of the story. It must not only be communicated early and often, but also clearly demonstrated throughout the business. When they understand the moral of the story and feel empowered to represent it, the story will be consistent and, as a result, stronger.

At Boston Medical Center, the moral permeates the walls of the entire facility. With the words prominently displayed in the building cafeteria where most every nurse, doctor, administrator, patient, family member, and donor eats, they are each reminded that life's greatest privilege is taking care of those around them. They know they belong, and every day they consider how they can demonstrate that. When a staff member sees someone looking confused or lost, he or she quickly runs over to help show the way. When a patient needs help that may not be available on campus, nurses and physicians do all they can to provide it. They find a way—and feel privileged to do it.

At DS SolidWorks, the moral can clearly be seen in the products themselves. Developers and engineers are constantly evolving the products to not only improve the sophistication of 3-D CAD but also enhance the ability for engineers to collaborate with one another. They recognize that people can create great things when they work together, like mobile and cloud-based products that enable engineers to design and share files virtually anywhere; integration with online file-sharing libraries and galleries that everyone in the community can access; and file formats that can be opened with virtually any software so everyone can work together seamlessly.

At Nurtury, prior to announcing the new brand name to the public, the organization's executive director, Wayne Ysaguire, stood in front of more than one hundred caregivers, administrators, board members, and community leaders and shared the story with them. He led each and every one of his team members through the journey we'd been on, preparing them for where they were heading.

It all made sense. To a person, everyone involved with the organization—many of whom were included in the process along the way—immediately understood why they were there, what the organization represented, and why the name change to Nurtury made sense. As the guests enjoyed the large cake decorated with the new brand logo and moral of the story, I listened to their excitement about the future of the organization and their role as nurturers.

Each and every time I witness an event like this one, I am reminded of the power of the moral. When the moral of the story truly captures the soul of a brand, that simple statement causes everyone in the room to immediately feel a connection with the brand they represent. They understand why the brand does what it does and understand how they are supposed to represent it.

But the communication cannot stop at the launch. Today, as you walk into the lobby of Nurtury's Learning Lab at Bromley Heath, you will be welcomed with the words "When you nurture a child, you nurture a community" on the wall in front you. All the staff members see those words every time they enter the building and every time they leave.

Throughout the Nurtury centers, posters on walls remind the employees—along with everyone else in the building—of why they are there. A picture of a young girl being held in the air by an adult is accompanied with a headline that reads, "She's learning to trust the laws of gravity. And those around her." Another image showing a mom next to a child says, "She's developing new skills. And her mom is developing new ways to teach her."

The annual gala is aptly called "A Night to Nurture," where they honor the Nurturer of the Year. And as Wayne stands up in front of everyone, he reminds them why they are there and what they can do to help.

Today, the entire staff at Nurtury know why they are there, and when performing their jobs can simply ask themselves, "What would someone whose core belief is 'when you nurture a child, you nurture a community' do?"

One of the most effective ways to help remind people of their role as brand storytellers is to have them think of themselves as something more than what their job title may suggest. At Nurtury, the team members are more than teachers, administrators, and board members. They are considered "Nurturers."

At The Base, Robert Lewis Jr. refers to his players, donors, partners, volunteers, and staff as "Believers." Each and every one of them recognizes that "if you believe you can, you can," and each is encouraged to help one another believe in themselves. At Small Army, we consider everyone a "Relationship Builder." Whether you are a project manager, art director, copywriter, producer, or intern, your job first and foremost is to help clients build relationships with people.

Brand representatives need more than a job description to understand their role. They must also understand their role as a brand storyteller.

It took many years and lots of self-reflecting for me to finally make sense of my role and purpose without Mike by my side. When we started Small Army in 2002, it had all seemed very clear. Our purpose was to help brands tell their story, and we each had defined roles to help us do that. It was the reason I thought we worked so well together. I was focused on business analytics and strategy, and Mike was the creative genius—the storyteller. We used to joke at meetings that I was the left side of the brain and Mike was the right side. Together, our clients got a full brain.

After Mike passed, I was lost. As I participated in client meetings and presentations, I couldn't help but notice his absence. Although I had other amazing creative professionals standing by my side, none of them were Mike. I could usually hold back my tears until I left the meeting, but every once in a while the feelings would overcome me. As time passed, I became better at containing my emotions and accepting the reality that Mike was not coming back.

As the agency got back into our groove, we began to make sense of everything that came before us. We launched Be Bold, Be Bald! We uncovered the moral of the story and a process for helping brands discover it. We honed our ability to apply the moral to help brands share their story. And the agency grew.

Eventually, when I finally thought I had it all together—intellectually and emotionally—I decided to do a TEDx Talk. I wanted to share how Mike inspired us to create Be Bold, Be Bald! and discover the moral of the story. For months, I worked endlessly to craft a speech that could tell the whole story in fifteen minutes or less. I wrote draft after draft, asking anyone willing to read it to provide feedback. My colleagues, my wife, and even my kids listened time and time again to each revision. And I worked with the leaders and volunteers from the TEDx group to hone the speech and my delivery. I wanted it to be perfect.

As the makeup artist applied concealer to my face and the audio technician helped me weave the microphone cord through my shirt, my fear turned into excitement. I was finally about to tell my story. John, the head of the conference, introduced me to the audience as I proudly walked out onto the big red dot in the center of the stage. I looked over the crowd of people from the stage, and suddenly I felt alone. I was about to share a story about my favorite storyteller and the journey we had taken together—and he wasn't there to share it with me. But as I looked into the audience and began speaking the words I had practiced over and over again, I could sense Mike watching over me with a smile. He was still with me, guiding me and helping me tell our story.

Walking off the stage, I felt relieved. I had done it. My wife came over and gave me a big hug, and the volunteers from the conference congratulated me on a job well done. I untucked the microphone, wiped off the makeup, and headed out to the lobby area. In the lobby, a young woman stopped me and said, "Mike may have been a great storyteller, but you just told a great story." At that moment, everything became clear. Mike was an amazing storyteller, but he actually did more than tell stories. He helped others become storytellers. Including me.

We are all storytellers. Every person who represents a brand is responsible for sharing its story. Marketing and communications professionals may be doing it in advertising, social media, websites, collateral, and other channels. However, product managers and engineers are sharing the story through the product. Store managers and associates are sharing the story through the retail experience. Cashiers, servers, and customer-service representatives are sharing the story with each and every interaction. Sales representatives are sharing the story in every pitch and follow-up. Financial executives are telling the story in financial reports, investor calls, and invoices. Everyone from the interns to the CEO is responsible for telling the brand story. Great brands require more than a great advertising campaign. They require that every person associated with the brand lives up to the brand story.

After many years of retrospection, I have come to discover that great brands are not the result of great products and services. Great products and services are simply the table stakes for success. The greatest brands—the ones we listen to, trust, and are loyal to—are those that share a story that people want to be a part of. They share a moral that people believe in and a happily-ever-after they all want to get to. They are consistent and relentlessly true to themselves. They encourage others to be a part of their story. And they empower everyone to share it.

When a brand discovers its moral, it has the power to share a great story, build strong relationships with people, and live on forever. Just like Mike.